Endorsements

From the opening quote ("S▪▪▪ *▪▪▪ ▪▪▪ ▪▪▪ you're
in—you're in. There's no gettin*▪ *▪▪▪ ▪▪▪ words ("I'll see
you in the water"), this may be not only one of the best books ever
written on surfing, but one of the best books ever written on what it
means to surf the Spirit as a disciple of Jesus. The moment I dipped
my toes into the book and "dropped in," I was so captivated by the
wisdom of the breaking waves and washing machine I didn't want to
"get out," even when I was washed ashore when I ran out of pages.*

– Leonard Sweet, best-selling author of *Bad Habits of Jesus*,
professor at Portland Seminary, Drew University, Tabor College,
and Evangelical Seminary, and founder of preachthestory.com

In his book, I Surf, Therefore I Am, *Philosopher Peter Kreeft
writes, "I think God surfs all the time." Another writer has commented,
"Life is a wave, and your attitude is your surfboard." I believe both.
If you've ever surfed, you know that it is truly a spiritual experience
that is almost beyond description. In* Dropping In, *Shane captures
the essence of all of this. With fun stories and insight into God and life
from the perspective that only a surfer can bring, this is a must-read
for anyone who has a bit of saltwater running through their veins.
Shane didn't just write this book—he lives it. I dare you to read it and
not have some of his spiritual stoke rub off on you.*

– Dr. Douglas Witherup, Lead Pastor, CFA Church
and Wanna-be Surfer

Jesus said, "I have come that they may have life, and have it to the full" (John 10:10). In his latest book, Dropping In, *Dr. Sebastian draws upon his experience of "spiritual stoke" in surfing to unpack for us what Jesus intended. This is a book about surfing and following Jesus, living over the ledge, trusting the wave, and placing our energy in what really matters.*

– Dr. Loren Kerns, Dean of Portland Seminary

Shane Sebastian knows surfing. Even more than surfing, Shane knows Jesus! Dropping In *takes you along on his many adventures and misadventures of surfing and following Jesus alike. This is the real-life tale of how God is using surfing to reveal himself to Shane and the world. Everyone who reads it, including wanna-be surfers like me, will want to jump on their surfboard and go after the biggest wave of their life...following Jesus!*

– Scott Rubin, Young Life Area Director North County San Diego

As an experienced surfer and minister, Shane invites us into the world of surfing and how to achieve spiritual stoke in our lives. Whether you are a surfer who wants to grow in your spiritual life or just a person surfing through life who wants more clarity on how to experience an abundant spiritual life, Dropping In *will help you have the direction you need to see God make more waves in your life, so that you can truly live a life of adventure and purpose.*

– Holly Melton, Speaker, Author of *Follow My Lead: Responding to God's Voice in Everyday Encounters*

Whether you surf or not, Dropping In *is a book for everyone. I really enjoyed reading all of Shane's stories and how he uses them to illustrate Biblical truth. This book is also an excellent resource for discipleship and small groups. I am certain anyone who reads this book will be inspired to share the beauty and "stoke" of life with Jesus!*

– Abel Mendez, Calvary Chapel, Student Ministries Pastor

If you have ever considered having spiritual influence through doing the things that you love, then Dropping In *is the book for you. Shane Sebastian shares refreshing stories and teaches with clarity on three of his favorite things: God, Family, and Surfing. If you are someone that likes to read stories of faith, family, and fun, but yet have powerful action steps for how to love God and love your life, then this is the book for you.*

– Gary Schmalz, Athletes in Action, Minneapolis

Shane has the unique gift of communicating life-changing truths in a down-to-earth way. Dropping In *is engaging, motivating, and brings a smile to the reader's soul.*

– Megan Donovan, Teaching Leader,
Bible Study Fellowship International, Parent

Dropping In *is an absolutely refreshing read. Dr. Sebastian hits the nail on the head and holds nothing back in giving us all the tools and resources we need to lead a deeper and fuller walk with Jesus. Surfers and non-surfers can expect to enjoy a well-rounded understanding of what it means to live a life filled with faith and spiritual stoke. To make this drop is to experience life fully refreshed and ready to take on any size wave this world may bring your way.*

– Aaron Gold, World Record Holder for Largest Wave Ever
Paddled, Professional Surfer, Actor in Surfers and Cowboys

Dropping In is a handbook for surfing the waves of the Spirit. I see people who are excited to learn to surf. They usually just run down to the beach and rent a surf board instead of hiring a beach boy to guide them. They struggle and often find themselves in peril. They do not know their way through the channels to get out to the take-off spot and when they get there they don't know what wave to catch, when to paddle, when to try to get up, and how to stand. They usually wipe-out or, worse, find themselves in serious danger.

Shane Sebastian's book is a guidebook for life. Its readability and adventurous stories draw the reader into a deeper contemplation of life, stirs up the desire to ride the waves of the Spirit and the wisdom to do so. Surfs Up!

– Bear Woznick, Best Selling Author, World Champion Tandem Surfer, Host of "Long Ride Home with Bear Woznick" EWTN Reality TV show, Host of "The Bear Woznick Adventure" EWTN Radio show, Founder of Deep Adventure Ministries

Shane does a great job using surf culture to introduce and invite his reader to live the adventure of following Jesus. His book is easy to read, very enjoyable, and relatable. It will definitely motivate you to know Jesus more and it may even inspire you to get out in the water!

– Jonathan Whitmore, Athletes in Action, Pacific Southwest

Dropping In is a revolutionary book. For years, Christian surfers have tried to express who Jesus is and how he can guide us in our daily lives. Dropping In has finally bridged the gap for surfers to grow closer to Jesus and better understand what life with him is all about.

– John Daniels, Retired Professional Surfer, Contest Judge, Coach, Owner of Learn to Rip Surf School

Shane Sebastian loves surfing and following Jesus, and his story reveals what it's like to do them both to the ends of the earth. Never having surfed, I learned a whole new vocabulary. But even more, what's so enjoyable is Shane's stories of surfing, which reveals that anyone can experience the stoke that comes from following Jesus.

– Keith Bubalo, Global Strategy Coordinator, The Jesus Film

Shane Sebastian loves surfing and loves Jesus, and his passion for both shines through on every page of Dropping In. *His contagious excitement will make you want to get in the water and get in the Word. Get ready for a ride... Shane Sebastian is the perfect guide for exploring the exhilarating world of life with Jesus.*

– Matt Mikalatos, speaker and author of
Good News for a Change: How to Talk to Anyone about Jesus

As an avid surfer and follower of Jesus, I've always enjoyed the similarities of our sport compared to our journey in Christ. In this book, Dr. Shane Sebastian has done a fantastic job doing just that. He's made a sometimes hard-to-relate subject fun, inviting, and easy-to-identify with. Even if you're not a surfer, this book will leave you super-stoked and ready to drop in!

– Randy Nolan, Founder of FLOW, Co-Director of Eco Pro Surf Series, Surf Brand Ambassador, Former National Champion & US Team member

Surfing is a great example of the Christian life; you have to be fully committed when you're putting faith in Jesus just like when you take that drop. A great read; I highly recommend this book to anyone of all ages.

– Gavin Seaman, Competitor Eastern Surfing Association, Lifeguard at Satellite Beach, FL

My surfing son gave me a love for the ocean—and for surfing. That is, watching others surf. Shane Sebastian has done a beautiful job of uniting the joy and thrill of riding waves with the joy and thrill of walking with Jesus. He makes it practical and enticing. Who wouldn't want to drop in on a perfect wave? And even better, who wouldn't want to connect with a perfect Friend and Savior? I will be getting this book for my son and my grandsons.

– Judy Douglass; Writer, speaker, encourager, Director, Women's Resources at Cru

Dropping In is a wave-riding description of what it means to follow Jesus with stoke. Shane writes with clarity and winsome skill, describing the Christian life through the brilliant metaphor of surfing. Don't miss the wave of Dropping In and get your copy today!

– Dr. Bryce Ashlin-Mayo; pastor, professor, and author of Age of Kings: Pursuing God's Heart in a Social Media World

Really cool to see Shane put to words what God has been showing me in the ocean all these years. If you are wondering why there is something more to the ocean but you can't quite put a finger on it, read Dropping In and have God, through Shane's experience, help you make that connection to fully experience the stoke that life and surfing have to offer.

– Damien Hobgood, Professional Surfer,
Big Wave World Tour Competitor

If you've ever wondered how to catch a wave this may be the best book you'll ever read. This is no self-help, Surfing for Dummies book. Dropping In is for you if you're looking to ride through the storms, "live for the line," learn to read the ocean of life, know when to paddle, and when to stand up. Even if you're a Grom, Shane offers ways to read and ride the waves of you life like a Kahuna on a longboard.

– Rev. Dr. Norbert Haukenfrers, Parish Priest in Okotoks, AB
and National Board Chair, Threshold Ministries, Canada

Dropping In

Experience the Life You Were Meant to Live

In

Shane Sebastian

Dropping In: Experience the Life You Were Meant to Live
By Dr. Shane Sebastian

Published by HigherLife Publishing and Marketing, Inc.
P.O. Box 623307, Oviedo, FL 32762
www.ahigherlife.com

ISBN Paperback: 978-1-7325026-8-0
ISBN Ebook: 978-1-7325026-9-7

Printed in the United States of America.

For my four children, Kirra, Summer, David, and Curren.

For my beautiful bride, Laura.

Thank you for riding the waves of life with me.

Many Thanks

Dropping In describes relationships — relationship with God and relationships with others. Surfing is an awesome sport and recreation, but surfing with my friends is what I enjoy most.

In Chapter One, I share the story of who introduced me to the sport of kings, Jim Rider. I am grateful, Jim, as you made me paddle out that day. Much more than that, I am grateful that you have been my best friend for over 35 years. Thank you for your integrity and example of a man who drops in and charges after the abundant life we are all promised.

I want to thank several men in my life, whom I continue surfing with since my childhood. Thanks to Jeff Mathis, Phil Larson, John Voris, Peter Hoyt, Cory Verner, and Brent Dunnam. Our trips over the years to Mexico and Latin America have been fun and so good for my soul. Sharing life with you is a gift.

My wife Laura and I love what we do, and we love the people who make it possible for us to reach out to others. I especially want to thank our team who sends us. A very special thanks to Tom and Karen Bellig, Tim and Stacy Williams, Jeremee and Nicole Pruitt, Stephen and Jennifer Allcott, Ken and Kristyn Krutenat, Randy and Sheryl Sherrod, John Bailey, Dick and Louise Kolb, Brent and Stephanie Dunnam and Dave and Teri Pearce.

Thank you, God, for giving me the opportunity to live the abundant life through Jesus.

The sound of the water is loud; the ocean waves are powerful, but the Lord above is much greater.

– Shane Sebastian

Table of Contents

Foreword

Is this a book about surfing? I'd say "yes and no". The cover photo seems to be about surfing. The name of the book, Dropping In, seems to be about surfing. The stories that Shane Sebastian shares so masterfully throughout the book seem to be about surfing. The people and places Shane references are legendary surfers and great surf spots. All evidence would point that this is a book about surfing. I guess you could say on the surface it is but I can tell you for certain, that as much as Shane loves surfing (and he really, really does love surfing), with his busy family life and a world of amazing experiences, he wouldn't have spent the time to simply write about book about surfing.

One of the distinguishing things about surfers is that we tend to obsess about it. Most people who enjoy a sport or recreational pursuit tend to focus a lot of their time, money and energy on that discipline. Basketball, soccer, skiing , biking; you name it. Those things certainly have their fan base and pursuers. But surfing is different. I used the word "obsessed" because it's the only word for it. Shane and I have recently become fast friends because we have a lot in common. Both of us lead mission organizations vocationally.

Shane has been a faithful leader in the ministry of Cru for years and I help lead a ministry called Christian Surfers. We have both been married about the same number of years and have kids almost the same age. We probably even have similar taste in music, books, and movies. We are also both surfers and have been most of our lives. Shane shares a lot about his obsession with surfing in this book. I can assure you my lifelong obsession with surfing is equally impressive or embarrassing depending on how you look at it. Even with our equal obsession with surfing, there is something we have in common that runs even deeper than surfing, which is why I know that this book isn't really about surfing.

Shane is a man who thinks much about faith, the mysteries of God, and his love for us. Shane has given much of his life in the pursuit of helping people try to understand what is certainly difficult to understand. My guess is that Shane can tell you countless stories of surfing and his surfing adventures. Many are recorded in this book, which makes it really fun and engaging to read. However, I'd bet you my favorite surfboard (which is really saying a lot because it's a great board) that Shane has even more stories of friends he has walked with on a journey to discover the great adventures of faith. This is why I know this book isn't really about surfing.

Some of the most important things in life seem to slip past the ability to simply use words to describe them. It's funny that I use the same word, "love", to describe how I feel about ice cream and how I feel about my children. I love ice cream but I love my children too even know I don't mean the same thing by the word "love". When it comes to trying to communicate great truths and even greater mysteries about faith, words alone seem just too slippery or bland to do the trick.

When Jesus spoke, we have recorded that he was a master storyteller. He told stories to communicate great truths and greater mysteries about faith. He knew that words alone wouldn't do the precepts justice. This is why Jesus himself was the master at using metaphor and analogies to communicate things that would be impossible for us to comprehend over time, and in different context and cultures. Jesus would say, "It (the Kingdom of God) is like…" Or, he would tell a metaphorical story, "there once was a woman who…".

Picture the followers of Jesus over two thousand years ago, gathered on a hillside or around the dinner table listening and learning from the one who is the living embodiment of truth, sharing in metaphors about things so deep and dear that words alone don't even come close to communicating the reality. Can you picture it? Everyone is leaning in because the stories themselves come alive when the master storyteller proclaims great truth with the simplest stories.

With Dropping In, God has used a most unlikely source to also share great truths about God and the adventure of faith that is possible to live. God has decided to use a surfer of all people to share stories about...well, surfing of course. However, Shane is not just sharing stories about surfing. Surfing is just the metaphor that Shane used with great skill and insight to share about the One that he is most passionate about in life. Although Shane is obsessed with surfing, I know his love for Jesus Christ consumes him and surfing has simply become a great tool to use to communicate. Frankly, reading Shane's stories about surfing and surfers is a lot of fun. So much so, that while I was reading this book (that isn't really about surfing) I found myself so glad I'm a surfer... but even more glad that I too am on a journey to understand the incredible opportunities offered on a journey of faith in Jesus Christ.

So if you are a surfer, you'll love this book because you'll think it is a book about surfing even though it isn't. And if you aren't surfer, you'll love this book because you'll learn all kinds of things about surfing. In fact, you can almost make this a textbook for learning to be a surfer, even though this book isn't a book about surfing. Either way, a surfer or a non-surfer, beginner or seasoned pro, you will learn that this book has so much to say about surfing and so much more to say about living a life of faith.

Shane has masterfully used the fun, true, authentic, adventurous, memorable, humorous, frightening, endearing, and real stories and metaphors of surfing to communicate what is truly life-changing. As you read this book and let it shape your thoughts, remember; this isn't a book about surfing. It is far too important to be just that. Enjoy Dropping In. Like a great wave, you'll be different when you get to the end.

- JW Kaiser, **President/National Director, Christian Surfers**

Introduction

"Vamonos, Shane! Vamonos! Salta al bote!"

"Let's go, Shane. Let's go! Get in the boat!"

It was a very warm morning just past five, one of my buddies and I were carrying our surfboards in waist deep water, and our boat driver was encouraging us to jump into his boat before the next set of waves arrived. After settling into our small Panga (a common boat in Central America), we motored around the point for the brief twenty-minute trip up the coast. It was going to be a great day of surfing.

The surface of the ocean was so clear and smooth it looked like glass. I was with one of my boys and a close friend. We saw dolphins in the distance, a solid four-foot swell was hitting the coast, and we were on the second day of an eight day dream trip to El Salvador. This was going to be the trip of a lifetime, right?

Wrong.

After surfing perfect waves for several hours, I paddled into a head high swell that peeled for well over one hundred yards. At the end of the wave, I slipped on the wax on my surfboard and wiped out. My right arm felt numb and tingly, and very painful at the same time.

I've fallen thousands of times over decades of surfing. This time, however, I fell in a way that dislocated my right shoulder. As I was literally dragged on the rocks I was able to "pop" my shoulder back into place. I struggled back to our boat and asked the driver to pull me up. We sped back to the hotel, and I jumped in a taxi and went to the nearest hospital an hour or so away. The pain, and then the doctor, was very clear in telling me that I would not be surfing again anytime soon. I booked the next flight home.

In a matter of seconds I went from the happiest person on the planet to feelings of disappointment, anger, and frustration.

Several days later I found myself in an office I would frequent often the next eight months — physical therapy. My doctor patiently taught me exercises that would help my shoulder heal. With the use of one-pound weights, stretching rubber bands, ice and heat treatment, and rest, my injury slowly (very slowly) rehabilitated. Throughout the process my physical therapist was very clear: there is no magic pill to healing. Do the exercises and rest. Do the exercises and rest. And again. And again. And again.

Over time the rotator cuffs, fibers, tendons, and muscles in my shoulder and upper back grew. Through all of the exercises I grew.

This book is written to help you grow. Over years of surfing and growing in a relationship with the creator of the waves, I want to provide you with exercises that can help you grow, too. The Bible is full of writings of rock solid wisdom that help us grow and live out the abundant life we are intended for.

This is a book about pursuing a life of purpose, deep meaning, connection, impact, and joy. This is a book about a term we will look at in Chapter One — Stoke.

If somewhere in the depth of your soul you long for more out of life than just playing it safe, getting by – existing, then this book is for you.

Despite what you may think, this book is not about surfing, well not primarily. It's about living the kind of exhilarating, thrilling, almost too-good-to-be-believed kind of life that's actually possible.

What surfing represents, and many surfers have experienced, is a feeling called "stoke." It's that happiness, that thrill and pure joy that comes when you catch and ride that perfect wave.

Believe it or not, God intends for you to have this kind of life. And yet so often we settle for much less. Dropping In will help you open your heart, mind, and soul to the possibility of living differently.

If standing on the shore of life has lost its appeal and you are ready to experience more, then you're ready to drop in and catch the wave of God's divine flow in your life that will keep you smiling.

Thanks for paddling out with me. Let's drop in together.

chapter
one
Spiritual Stoke

Surfer pictured: Mick Fanning

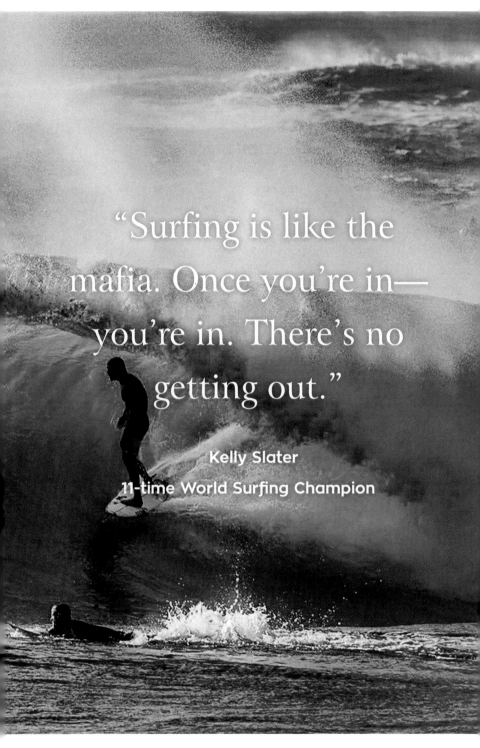

"Surfing is like the mafia. Once you're in— you're in. There's no getting out."

Kelly Slater

11-time World Surfing Champion

I grew up forty-five minutes from the ocean. Most of my summers were spent going to the beach. I would hitch rides with my family, our church youth group, public transportation, or my friends. One afternoon, after my freshman year of college, my best friend and I drove to our favorite beach in North County, outside San Diego.

As usual, we stopped at the Solana Beach Donut House and ate a ridiculous amount of sugar, downed it all with a healthy Mountain Dew, and rushed out of the car to retrieve our boards. At this point in surfing, I was still bodysurfing and bodyboarding. Before I had time to change into my wetsuit, my friend Jim locked my bodyboard in the cab of his truck and gave me his extra surfboard. Jim looked at me and said in no uncertain terms, "Too bad, Shane. No bodyboarding for you this time. Today you are going to stand up."

I am forever indebted to Jim.

A short time later, I nervously, yet expectantly, sat outside of the breaking surf waiting for a wave. A smaller set of waves approached. I paddled, felt the wave begin to catch me, and jumped to my feet. Though I probably looked like a kook (more on that word later in the book), I felt like I was the best surfer in the world. I rode the wave for perhaps four or five seconds, kicked out, and immediately looked around to see if anyone had seen my wave (unfortunately, no one did).

Dropping in that wave was like nothing I had ever experienced. I was hooked. After several hours of surfing (for me, it was mostly paddling), the sun dipped below the horizon. As I rode my last wave to shore, I felt a strong sense of joy, exhilaration, and contentment. You may have heard the quote: "Only a surfer knows the feeling."

That feeling is what a surfer refers to as stoke.

"Surfing is simply the most fun I know how to have on this planet." - Antony Lisi

Ask a surfer what stoke means and you will likely receive various answers: happiness, fulfillment, pure joy, excitement, fun. In John 10:10, Jesus Christ speaks of what I like to refer to as spiritual stoke. He says, "My purpose is to give them a rich and satisfying life." In other translations, the word abundant is used to express what Jesus wants to give his children in life.

I love that. Jesus Christ came to the world to give people a rich, abundant, and satisfying life. To be spiritually stoked is to experience the abundance, the richness, and the satisfaction

---

To be spiritually stoked is to experience the abundance, the richness, and the satisfaction God desires for you.

God desires for you. This stoke, whether you consider yourself a surfer or not, is what God wants for you.

I have four groms. The term grom is an affectionate word used for kids who love to surf. I think of several times my groms have been stoked. Several years ago, my wife and I surprised our son David with a new surfboard for his birthday. His expression was pure stoke. I remember last year, his twin sister, Summer, received a new bike on Christmas. She had joy and excitement written all over her face.

My oldest daughter, Kirra, recently joined me on a business trip to Europe. When I told her she was coming with me, she was so stoked I thought she would fall over. And finally, I will never forget pushing my youngest son, Curren, into his first wave. We were living in Puerto Rico at the time. I swam out with him at a beautiful beach called Maria's. A small wave approached, I gently pushed him, he jumped to his feet and rode it to shore. It took several hours for his smile to fade. Curren was so full of joy even I could feel it.

God wants us to enjoy the life he has given us. He wants our lives to be meaningful, abundant, and rich. He wants us to experience spiritual stoke.

Walking on Water

"Surfing can be a religious experience."
– Tom Curren, World Champion

The Bible speaks often of the sea and its powerful waves. Throughout the four books of the Bible that give different views of the life of Jesus (the Gospels), we see Jesus spend much of his time in or near the Sea of Galilee. He spent time there by himself in prayer and solitude, he spent time there with his close friends, and he spent time in or near the sea teaching, and sometimes even healing, crowds of people.

The book of Psalms shares much of God's creation and the ocean. *Who stills the roaring of the seas, the roaring of their waves, and the tumult of the peoples?* (Psalm 65:7, NASB) Psalm 93:4 says, *More than the sounds of many waters, than the mighty breakers of the sea, the Lord on high is mighty* (NASB). In the book of Isaiah, we see the power of God and his might compared to the ocean: *For I am the Lord your God, who stirs up the sea and its waves roar* (Isaiah 51:15, NASB).

Throughout the Bible, we read that Jesus and the sea often go together. Below is the well-known story of Jesus coming to the aid of his friends by literally walking on water and calming the stormy waves.

> *Immediately after this, Jesus insisted that his disciples get back into the boat and cross to the other side of the lake, while he sent the people home. After sending them home, he went up into the hills by himself to pray. Night fell while he was there alone. Meanwhile, the disciples were in trouble far away from land, for a strong wind had risen, and they were fighting heavy waves. About three o'clock in the morning Jesus came toward them, walking on the water. When the disciples saw him walking on the water, they were terrified. In their fear, they cried out, "It's a ghost!" But Jesus spoke to them at once. "Don't be afraid," he said. "Take courage. I am here!" Then Peter called to him, "Lord, if it's really you, tell me to come to you, walking on the water." "Yes, come," Jesus said. So Peter went over the side of the boat and walked on the*

water toward Jesus. But when he saw the strong wind and the waves, he was terrified and began to sink. "Save me, Lord!" he shouted. Jesus immediately reached out and grabbed him. "You have so little faith," Jesus said. "Why did you doubt me?"   - Matthew 14:23-32 (NLT)

I love this story. As the sun is setting, we find Jesus spending time in the hills praying while his friends fish nearby in the Sea of Galilee. A powerful storm slams the sea, creating large waves that threaten the lives of Jesus' friends. Jesus came to the rescue by walking on water toward the boat. One of Jesus' best friends, a very emotional leader named Peter, steps out in faith and obedience (as Jesus tells him to "come") and also walks on water. When Peter doubts Jesus, he begins to sink, and when he believes in Jesus, he is able to walk on water.

In this story, we see Jesus calm the waves and display his power. While he does this, he shows us his desire for Peter to trust and obey him. How exactly does Jesus do this? Jesus invites Peter to come to him, to trust him, to walk with him. But there is a catch here. To do so, Peter needs to get out of the boat. Jesus will take care of Peter, even in the middle of a powerful storm that was frightening the most seasoned of fishermen. But first, Peter needs to get out of the boat.

You are holding a book that encourages you to get out of the boat. This is a book that will hopefully point you toward and strengthen you in a trusting relationship with the one who walked on water, calmed the ocean's waves, and looked out for his friends.

Experiencing an abundant life, spiritual stoke, does not come from living an easy, comfortable life. Jesus does not promise a stress-free life. But Jesus does promise abundant life. This spiritual stoke is a life thoroughly enjoyed in the context of a relationship with the God who created you, the God who created the mighty waves of the ocean, the God who desires to walk with you.

Living for the Line

Though I didn't start surfing until I was in my late teens, I grew up fascinated by waves and the ocean. This love for the sea was on my mind as I considered college. I went to college at the University of California, Irvine. I chose UC Irvine because of its proximity to the ocean in Southern California. Newport Beach borders UC Irvine, and as any California surfer knows, Newport has some awesome surfing.

I was strategic when choosing my class schedule each quarter as a college student. I kept my mornings wide open to allow for maximum surf time, I went to class (well, most of the time) in the afternoon, and I had a part-time job a few evenings each week.

One morning after surfing a fun south swell at Newport River Jetties, I met with my friend Alex on campus. After a less-than-fulfilling Taco Bell burrito (I ate thousands of those during college), Alex read me this Bible verse that radically impacted my life: *Since you have been raised to new life with Christ, set your sights on the realities of heaven* (Colossians 3:1, New Living Translation).

Alex explained that the Bible speaks of living for things that will outlive us, for things that truly matter, for the nonmaterial. Alex then drew a line in the dust on the table in front of us. He said, "Shane, this line represents eternity; this line represents all of time. Where would you place your life on this line?"

I thought about it for a minute. If I'm lucky, I'll live seventy or eighty, maybe even ninety, years. In light of eternity, that was only a small fraction of the line drawn in front of me. I looked at Alex and said, "Well, I would represent my life with this dot." I placed a tiny dust dot on that table.

Alex then asked me a question I will never forget: "Okay, Shane, do you want to live for that small dot or do you want to live for the entire line?"

I looked at Alex and told him, in no uncertain terms, that I wanted to live for the line. I want to live, to invest my life in things that will outlive me.

How about you? Do you want to live for the dot or do you want to live for the line? A mentor of mine in graduate school,

---

Every person decides whether their footprints will last beyond a lifetime or sink in the sands of time.

---

author Leonard Sweet, shared this quote that has stuck with me for years: "Every person decides whether their footprints will last beyond a lifetime or sink in the sands of time." Living for the line means the footprints we make will be cemented into eternity, not washed away by the waves of life.

Dropping In is all about living for the line. As you read this book, you will be encouraged and practically guided on what it means to live not just for the dot of your life but for the entire line of eternity.

Dropping In is a book about surfing and following Jesus. This is a book about so much more than looking for and dropping in the perfect wave. I trust what you have in your hands will not just point you to good waves but to the good God who desires to bless you with even more than the joy of surfing.

No matter where you are in your spiritual journey, I hope you enjoy reading *Dropping In* and, more importantly, that it helps you grow in your relationship with the creator of the waves. You will read stories of surfing and how God has used this fun sport to encourage me in different aspects of the Christian life. Prayer, friendship, forgiveness, commitment, and understanding God's purpose for our lives are just a few of the topics we will address together.

To drop in means to commit without fully understanding what will happen. *Dropping In* means stepping out in faith and obedience, not knowing exactly where the wave will take you, and allowing God to shape and grow you in a relationship with him. *Dropping In* means taking the words of Jesus seriously, experiencing spiritual stoke, and walking on water with him throughout life. I trust this book will be a resource that helps shape and grow your relationship with Jesus.

You ready? Great. Wax up your board, slap on some sunscreen, start to paddle, jump to your feet, and let's drop in together.

Questions for
Personal or Group Reflection

1. What does dropping in mean?

2. What is spiritual stoke?

3. How do dropping in and spiritual stoke relate to one another?

4. How will you drop in to your relationship with God?

chapter
two
Going Over the Ledge

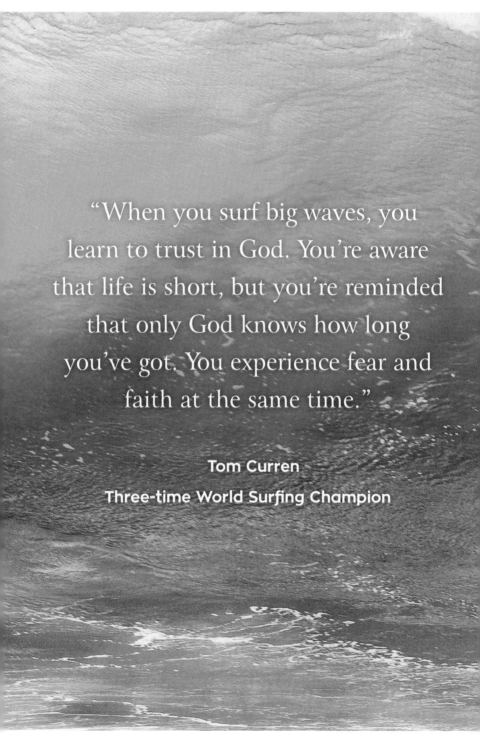

"When you surf big waves, you learn to trust in God. You're aware that life is short, but you're reminded that only God knows how long you've got. You experience fear and faith at the same time."

Tom Curren
Three-time World Surfing Champion

The scene was like one I had dreamed of since I was a kid in school and looking at old surfing magazines. I was in the middle of the South Pacific Ocean, surfing a right-hand reef pass in front of our hotel. The water was beyond clear. So clear it was like there was nothing between the bottom of the ocean and the surfboard I was sitting on. A few hundred yards behind me was Viti Levu, the main island in the Fijian Island chain. In front of me was one of the largest waves I had seen since arriving with my wife, Laura, and infant daughter, Kirra. The sun was setting, our flight back to the mainland was leaving in four hours, and our bus to the airport was waiting.

I hesitated as the overhead wave approached. The water was shallow, perhaps less than three or four feet deep over sharp coral reef. The last thing I needed was reef rash, stitches, or anything that may delay our trip home.

But I had to go. The wave was perfect. If I backed off and allowed my fear to keep me from going, I knew I would regret it.

I dug my arms deep into the water, paddling as hard as I could to get into the beautiful swell. As I felt the wave's momentum, I jumped to my feet and threw myself over the ledge.

I barely made it to the bottom of the wave, feeling the fins of my board catch the water while I turned and raced for open water. I watched the reef underneath me, dragged my right arm in the side of the wave for balance and control, and focused my eyes on the safety of the channel. I kicked out, looked to the sky, and raised my arms up with stoke.

I surfed that wave over fifteen years ago and it lasted no longer than seven or eight seconds, but I remember it like it happened yesterday.

It was an amazing ride, though I paid the price. Several waves behind it had broken and were coming straight for me as I tried to paddle to shore. When the whitewash hit me, I scraped against the reef, resulting in several cuts and bruises on my legs and ankle. On top of that, my board received several dings that were likely beyond repair.

Surfers call this scenario "getting worked." Let's just say I got thoroughly beat up. I was content and stoked with that final wave, but at the same time, I was tired and struggling to get to the beach.

By dropping in that wave, I experienced joy and stoke. I also experienced injury and insult. But I am so glad I dropped in; if I would have backed off, I wouldn't have experienced the speed, the tube, and the exhilaration of surfing a six-foot right-hand reef pass. Dropping in—going over the ledge—brought adventure and contentment. Dropping in also brought anxiety, stress, and pain.

In a lot of ways this is a metaphor for the Christian life.

Following Jesus—dropping in—is the beginning of a lifetime adventure of walking through life with the creator of the universe.

Following Jesus—dropping in—is the beginning of a lifetime

adventure of walking through life with the creator of the universe. This brings exhilaration and purpose, blessings and joy, contentment and peace. However, dropping in also brings challenges. The Christian life, following Jesus, is not a life free from trials and tribulations. No, the Christian life is one that helps us address them.

As we begin this book, let's take a deeper look at how we take the initial drop of following Jesus. What and how do we drop in, throw ourselves over the ledge, and begin that life of walking with him?

The Foundation of Spiritual Stoke

A few years ago, I was surfing a fun little wave called Pools on the northwest corner of Puerto Rico. A few minutes into my surf session, I began to trade waves and talk with a local ripper (a ripper is what we call a very good surfer who lives near that beach). We spoke of life and family and he asked me what I did as a career. I told him about my job with the local universities in Puerto Rico. I explained that I met with students to share with them how they can know and walk with the God who loves them. I shared more about the Bible studies that I led on campuses and how I would partner and serve with local churches in the area to help people know and grow with God.

As we talked and surfed together, I was struck with the simple yet profound truth that there is a God who desires to be in relationship with his creation, with you and me. To begin that relationship God desires to have with you, there are four things to understand. In other words, here is how to initially drop in.

Truth #1: Dropping In Begins with God's Love

On February 3rd, 2000, I was surfing Devereux Point just west of Santa Barbara. I remember that surf session clearly because when I arrived at my car, I had several voicemails from my wife that said, "Where are you? I'm in labor!"

When your wife is in labor, you change out of your four-millimeter wetsuit and booties as fast as possible, toss your surfboard in your truck, don't say goodbye to your friends who have yet to walk in from the beach, and you forget that you were hungry and planning to get a burrito.

When your wife is in labor with your first child (well, any child for that matter), you forget everything and race to the hospital.

Early the next morning, I looked deep into the eyes of Kirra, born a healthy little grom of 6 pounds and 10 ounces. I have a deep love for my daughter and for my other three children. The first time I held each of my kids, I was completely overwhelmed with love for them; it's an intense and affectionate love that is almost unexplainable.

The love that I have for my children pales in comparison to the love that God has for you and me. The Bible is full of stories and verses of God's deep, affectionate, and unstoppable love for you. In Psalm 86:15, the Bible says, *But you, O Lord, are a God merciful and gracious, slow to anger and abounding in steadfast love and faithfulness* (ESV). Psalm 136:12 says, *His steadfast love endures forever.* Zephaniah 3:17 says, *The Lord your God is in your midst, a mighty one who will save; he will rejoice over you with gladness; he will quiet you by his love; he will exult over you with loud singing* (ESV).

To begin a relationship with God, we realize that God loves us and desires to know us personally, forever. We read this in John 17:3: *And this is eternal life, that they know you the only true God, and Jesus Christ whom you have sent* (NASB). We also come to understand that God has an abundant plan for our lives, as Jesus says in John 10:10: *"I came that they may have life and have it abundantly"* (NASB). This abundant life, spiritual stoke as explained earlier, is living a life in relationship with the God who created you.

Truth #2: The Problem - Our Separation

One day after class at UC Irvine, I rushed down to the pier at Huntington Beach to go surfing. My friends had told me the waves were good, it was getting late, and I had perhaps another hour of daylight left. I frantically changed into my wetsuit, ran down to the south end of the pier, jumped into the ocean, and paddled out. I kicked out of my first wave and jumped off my surfboard, only to realize that it was not attached to my ankle. It was now surfing itself all the way to the beach. In the midst of my excitement and rushing to the water, I had forgotten to attach the leash of my surfboard to my ankle. It was very frustrating being separated from my surfboard at the beginning of my surf session.

The Bible teaches that God loves us and wants to be in a relationship with us. However, we have a problem that separates us from beginning this relationship. This problem is what the Bible refers to as sin. Romans 3:23 says, *For all have sinned and fall short of the glory of God.* Romans 6:23 says, *For the wages of sin is death, but the free gift of God is eternal life in Christ Jesus our Lord* (ESV).

God created us to be in fellowship with him. Because of our sin, we chose to go our own way and this fellowship with God was broken. This self-will, which can be characterized by an

---

This self-will, which can be characterized by an attitude of passive indifference or active rebellion, is what the Bible calls sin.

---

attitude of passive indifference or active rebellion, is what the Bible calls sin.

When the Bible was written, the word sin was used in archery. When someone would shoot an arrow and miss the bullseye, the perfect mark, the scorekeeper would yell out, "Sin!" Sin simply means imperfection, missing the mark of perfection.

God is holy and perfect. Our sin, our imperfection, keeps us from knowing him. No amount of work can earn us God's favor. Something unique to Christianity, which I especially appreciate, is that it is the only worldview that does not require we work for our salvation. Every other religion in history claims that there are certain ways to live and work, and duties to be done, in order to become right with God.

Laird Hamilton has always been one of my favorite surfers. Hamilton is from the outer island of Kauai. He is a modern big wave pioneer, an early pioneer of tow-in surfing (being pulled into giant waves behind a personal watercraft), and is accomplished in windsurfing, waterskiing, and kitesurfing. He even makes great coffee! To his very core, Hamilton is connected to the ocean. Only fish feel more comfortable in the water than Laird Hamilton.

However, if you told Laird to swim from his native Kauai to Japan, he would only get a certain distance before drowning— he can only go so far on his own. As strong as he is, and even with his superior swimming skills, there is no way he could survive. It's just not possible. He would swim much further than I would, but there is no possible way he could swim his way through the Pacific Ocean to Japan.

The Bible teaches that no matter how good we are, how well we live, there is no possible way to work our way to heaven. We are born into sin. We are born imperfect and that keeps us from knowing God.

Truth #3: The Very Good News

"Get up, Shane! It's so good out there! We finally have waves!"

My friends and I were at the end of a weekend surf trip south of Rosarito, Mexico. We had left for a camping trip on the beach a few days prior and were expecting big waves with pristine conditions. However, we had been "skunked" and had not surfed the waves we hoped for. Our last night, we went to bed feeling discouraged about heading home the next morning.

That last morning, as my buddies screamed about the awesome waves, I jumped out of my sleeping bag and stumbled over the sand dune with a cup of coffee. I looked out to see a solid four- to six-foot south swell lighting up the coast. It was a beautiful sight after looking at a flat ocean the previous few days. The view was very good news to a group of surf-starved teenagers.

You may have heard Christianity described as "the good news." To understand this good news is to realize several things about God:

1. **Jesus Died in Our Place.** This good news is that Jesus died in our place to cover our sin, to cover our imperfection. Romans 5:8 says, *But God shows his love for us in that while we were still sinners, Christ died for us* (ESV). We cannot earn our way to God because of our sin, because of our imperfection. God in his love recognizes this and reaches down to us to make a way for us to know him. This is very good news!

2. **Jesus Rose from the Dead.** Jesus not only died for our sins, but he rose from the dead. We read this in 1 Corinthians 15:3-6: *Christ died for our sins...He was buried... He was raised on the third day, according to the Scriptures...He appeared to Peter, then to the twelve. After that he appeared to more than five hundred people.* Also, in 1 Peter 3:18, *Christ suffered for our sins for all time. He never sinned, but he died for sinners to bring you safely home* (NLT).

3. **Jesus Is the Only Way to God.** We read this in John 14:6: *Jesus told him, "I am the way, the truth, and the life. No one comes to the Father except through me."* Jesus is not a way

to God along with being a good person, going to church on Sundays, or praying every morning. Jesus is the way to God.

Think back to the previous illustration about Laird Hamilton and me swimming from the shores of Kauai to Japan. We could never make it to Japan by ourselves. Even a waterman like Hamilton could not do this by himself. But if someone picked us up on a boat, fed us, gave us shelter and passage, we could get there.

God does this for us. He knows we can't make it to heaven without him. He understands we could never work our way into a relationship with him. How much work would be enough? How good is good enough to be in relationship with the God of the universe? It's impossible unless we are perfect. In light of this, he reaches down to us through his son Jesus Christ and makes a way for us. God has bridged the gulf that separates us from him by sending his son, Jesus, to die on a cross in our place to pay the penalty for our sins. Again, this is the good news.

It's not enough to intellectually know and agree with these points. The final point is one of action and decision, one where you can change the course of your eternity, one where you begin your experience of spiritual stoke. This is where you decide to drop in and begin a relationship with God.

Truth #4: It's Your Decision

Several years ago, my wife and kids surprised me with a surfboard for my birthday. Opening my eyes and having my son hand me a brand-new FireWire surfboard was so exciting. It was exciting because it was free and new and would help me to surf better. I was beyond stoked to receive this gift.

The Bible teaches that knowing God and all the benefits that come with this relationship is a free gift. We do nothing to earn this gift of a relationship with God. We don't deserve to be forgiven of our sins and have eternal life. It's not something we have to earn. Once we receive Jesus Christ as Savior and Lord, we can know and experience God's love and his plan for our lives. To experience this free gift and begin a relationship with God, we understand and act on four things:

1. **We Must Receive Christ.** Jesus explains this in John 1:12 when he says, *"But as many as received Him, to them He gave the right to become children of God, even to those who believe in His name"* (NASB).

2. **We Receive Christ Through Faith.** Ephesians 2:8-9 says, *"For by grace you have been saved through faith. And this is not your own doing; it is the gift of God, not a result of works, so that no one may boast"* (ESV). This gift is free. To begin this relationship with God, you place your faith in Jesus alone.

3. **When We Receive Jesus, We Experience a New Birth.** In John chapter 3, Jesus speaks to a religious leader named Nicodemus.

> *Now there was a man of the Pharisees named Nicodemus, a ruler of the Jews. This man came to Jesus by night and said to him, "Rabbi, we know that you are a teacher come from God, for no one can do these signs that you do unless God is with him." Jesus answered him, "Truly, truly, I say to you, unless one is born again he cannot see the kingdom of God." Nicodemus said to him, "How can a man be born when he is old? Can he enter a*

second time into his mother's womb and be born?" Jesus answered, "Truly, truly, I say to you, unless one is born of water and the Spirit, he cannot enter the kingdom of God. That which is born of the flesh is flesh, and that which is born of the Spirit is spirit. Do not marvel that I said to you, 'You must be born again.' The wind blows where it wishes, and you hear its sound, but you do not know where it comes from or where it goes. So it is with everyone who is born of the Spirit" (ESV).

In this conversation with Nicodemus, Jesus speaks of being born again. Like all of us, Nicodemus was born once already, born into sin, born corrupt, and born distant from God. But Jesus speaks here of a new birth, a new life with new aim and purpose. Jesus introduces this expression, being "born again," to powerfully illustrate the change that takes place in our lives after receiving Christ.

4. **We Receive Jesus by Personal Invitation.** I love how Jesus uses the metaphor of a door and knowing him in Revelation 3:20 when he says, *"Behold, I stand at the door and knock. If anyone hears my voice and opens the door, I will come in to him and eat with him, and he with me"* (ESV). Recently, I was showing a friend how he could experience a relationship with God. I explained to him that the door Jesus speaks of in this verse represents our hearts, our lives, and our minds. The handle to this door is only on the inside. God is not going to force himself on us. The decision to accept Christ is ours. Jesus is standing outside the door of your heart, the door of your life, right now, and he is knocking. Jesus knocks and waits. He wants to be in relationship with you.

Jesus is knocking on the door of your heart and life right now. Will you open it?

One evening when we were out to dinner, I remember asking my neighbor, "If you were to die today, what would you say are your chances of going to heaven?"

He answered, "I don't know, Shane, perhaps seventy-five or eighty percent."

I said, "Okay, Mike, would you like to be one hundred percent sure like me?"

His answer was immediate. "Of course I would."

I went on to share with Mike that we can be one-hundred percent sure we will go to heaven. The Bible is clear that if we accept Jesus Christ as our Lord and Savior, we will not only begin a relationship with him, but we will go to heaven. I invited him to pray with me, and he prayed to become a Christian with me right then and there in the restaurant.

I ask you the same question I asked my buddy Mike. Would you pray and receive Christ right now?

Prayer is simply talking with God. You can talk to God out loud (which I do all the time when I am surfing), or you can talk to God in the quietness of your own heart. God knows your heart and is not as concerned with your words as he is with the attitude of your heart. The following is a suggested prayer:

"Lord Jesus, I need you and I want to be in relationship with you. Thank you for dying on the cross for my sins. I open the door of my life, the door of my heart and mind, to you right now and receive you as my Savior and my Lord. Thank you for forgiving my sins and giving me eternal life. Take control of my life. Make me the kind of person you want me to be. Amen."

Does this prayer express the desire of your heart? Could you say this prayer and mean it? If so, I encourage you right now to pray this prayer and become a follower of Jesus.

If you just asked Jesus to come into your life, many things have already happened:

1. You can be certain that Jesus is in your life. Jesus states clearly that if we open the door of our hearts, he will enter (Revelation 3:20).

2. You have eternal life. The Bible says that those who have Christ have eternal life. We read this in 1 John 5:11-15: *And this is the testimony, that God gave us eternal life, and this life is in his Son. Whoever has the Son has life; whoever does not have the Son of God does not have life. I write these things to you who believe in the name of the Son of God that you may know that you have eternal life. And this is the confidence that we have toward him, that if we ask anything according to his will he hears us. And if we know that he hears us in whatever we ask, we know that we have the requests that we have asked of him* (ESV). As the end of this passage says, we can be confident that we have eternal life, because we have asked him into our lives.

3. Your sins are forgiven. We read this in Colossians 1:13-14: *He has delivered us from the domain of darkness and transferred us to the kingdom of his beloved Son, in whom we have redemption, the forgiveness of sins* (ESV).

4. You became a child of God. John 1:12-13 teaches, *But to all who did receive him, who believed in his name, he gave the right to become children of God, who were born, not of blood nor of the will of the flesh nor of the will of man, but of God* (ESV).

5. You have begun an amazing adventure as a new creation. In 2 Corinthians 5:17 it says, *Therefore, if anyone is in*

Christ, he is a new creation. The old has passed away; behold, the new has come (ESV).

Next Steps

One day when I was on campus in Puerto Rico, I met a student named Juan-Carlos. A few days earlier, Juan-Carlos had filled out a survey for me about spiritual things. As I spoke with him about his religious background and his life story, I asked him if he would have thirty minutes to talk more about what it means to have a relationship with God through the person of Jesus Christ. I remember thinking, "This kid doesn't want to talk to me and he doesn't want to talk about Jesus."

I was wrong.

After an hour of conversation, Juan-Carlos prayed and became a follower of Jesus, right there in the cafeteria on campus. That afternoon, we surfed a very fun reef-break together near his university. This was the beginning of a new relationship where I was able to see Juan-Carlos grow as a new creation. Since that time, Juan-Carlos has brought his friends to church, prays for his friends on a daily basis, and has seen one of his friends come into a relationship with Jesus. I was recently with Juan-Carlos's parents and they told me that their son has become a model to them as he walks with Jesus.

When Juan-Carlos became a Christian, I shared with him this very simple plan to begin to grow in his new relationship with God, GROWTH. This is taken from my favorite website that I recommend to new and growing followers of Jesus: www.startingwithGod.com

Go—Go to God in prayer each day. *If you abide in me, and my words abide in you, ask whatever you wish, and it will be done for you.* - John 15:7

Read—Read the Bible each day. *Now these Jews were more noble than those in Thessalonica; they received the word with all eagerness, examining the Scriptures daily to see if these things were so.* - Acts 17:11

Obey—Obey God moment by moment. *Whoever has my commandments and keeps them, he it is who loves me. And he who loves me will be loved by my Father, and I will love him and manifest myself to him.* - John 14:21

Witness—Point others toward God through your life and words. *And he said to them, "Follow me, and I will make you fishers of men."* - Matthew 4:19 *By this my Father is glorified, that you bear much fruit and so prove to be my disciples.* - John 15:8

Trust—Trust God for every detail in your life. *Humble yourselves, therefore, under the mighty hand of God so that at the proper time he may exalt you, casting all your anxieties on him, because he cares for you.* - 1 Peter 5:6-7

Holy Spirit—Allow God to control and live through your daily life. *But I say, walk by the Spirit, and you will not gratify the desires of the flesh.* - Galatians 5:16

If you prayed the prayer above, I want to say congratulations on dropping in, on jumping over the ledge, on becoming a child of God. As you grow in your new relationship with God, you will experience the abundant life, the spiritual stoke that God promises.

Questions for
Personal or Group Reflection

1. What does it mean to drop in on a spiritual level?

2. How do we initially drop in and begin a relationship with God?

3. What has already happened if you asked Jesus into your heart?

4. What is GROWTH?

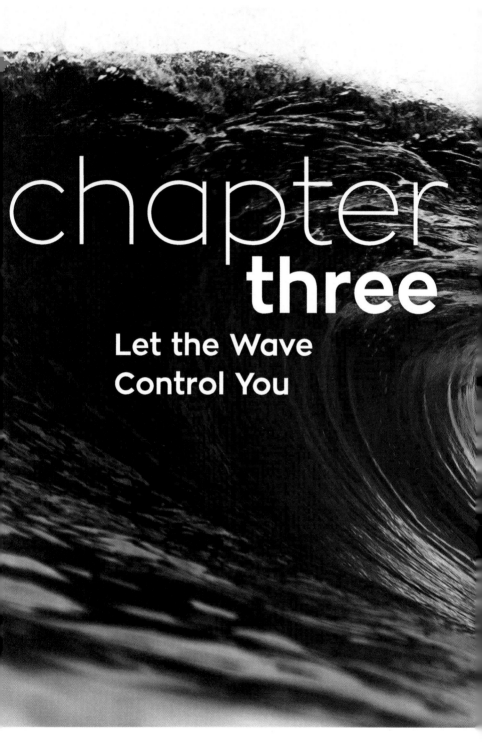

chapter
three

Let the Wave
Control You

"I could not help concluding this man had the most supreme pleasure while he was driven so fast and so smoothly by the sea."

Captain James Cook

Each summer, my family and I return to Southern California to visit friends and family. We love going back to where we have spent most of our lives, attending the church that has been such a source of encouragement to us, and being reminded of where we came from.

There is also one other reason, a very important reason, we like to spend time in Southern California: the surfing.

The pointbreaks of Santa Barbara, the beachbreaks of Newport, Huntington Beach and San Clemente, and the laid back vibe of Oceanside provide endless opportunities to catch fun waves. There is a particular place in Oceanside we love to surf as a family, and we do so as often as we can.

Last summer, our plane landed in San Diego late on a weekday morning. No less than two hours later, after securing our rental car and driving forty-five minutes north, my boys and I had our wetsuits on and were paddling out into solid four to six foot surf at our favorite surf spot. This day, as is true of many June days, had a solid south swell running.

From May through September, waves in Southern California are generated by large storms in the South Pacific near New Zealand. To the delight of surfers, large south swells march several thousands of miles across the ocean and unload onto the miles and miles of beaches in Southern California. As I paddled out with my sons, I said a prayer of gratitude for these south swells.

These swells also produce rip currents that make it difficult to be in a position to catch a good wave. After thirty minutes, I grew more and more frustrated as I was unable to catch a wave. I paddled up and down the beach trying so hard to drop in to a good swell. When I finally rode my first wave, I fell doing a turn that I normally complete with ease.

I was annoyed with myself, the ocean, and the fact that I had been in the water for so long without catching anything fun. I was trying so hard to surf well. In a way, I was forcing my surfing and trying to control everything around me. Instead of allowing the wave to guide and control where I was going, I was trying to guide and control the wave. As soon as I realized this and allowed the power of the wave to control my movements, I began to enjoy my surf session. I exited the water a few hours later refreshed and stoked.

The Christian Life is Not about Trying

The Christian life is very similar to that surf session. When I go surfing and try to control the wave, I find myself frustrated and feeling defeated. However, when I give control to the power of the wave, I am able to surf the wave to the

When I allow God to control my thoughts and actions, I am content and fulfilled in where and who he has called me to be.

fullest of my potential. In life, when I attempt to control my circumstances and force things to go my way, I normally end up frustrated, feeling defeated, and unfulfilled (and this seems to happen quite often). However, when I allow God to control my thoughts and actions, I am content and fulfilled in where and who he has called me to be.

My friend, Keith Bubalo, writes of this in his book, *Go, Do, Say, Give: The Freedom and Fruitfulness of Surrender to Jesus.*

> *"For many, being a Christian is a life that is defined by words like self-effort, commitment, and trying harder. Don't get me wrong. Of course, there is a need for discipline and determination in the Christian life. God has given us, as his children, this desire to work hard and do our best. Yielding to Jesus as Lord is saying you want to love and follow him without reservation, with no disclaimers or hesitations. But the question we need to ask is, where do we get the power in our lives in accordance with that desire? We must know and understand that it comes from God himself, through the person of the Holy Spirit who dwells within every true believer. He has not left us alone on our journey."*

As we walk with Jesus throughout life, God gives us the fulfillment, the freedom, and the stoke to live a life that is pleasing to him. The most practical way we can do this is to be filled with God's Spirit, the Holy Spirit. This book is written to help you connect to God in your daily life. I believe that understanding who the Holy Spirit is, why the Holy Spirit came, and how we can be filled with the Holy Spirit is the most important daily thing we can do as believers to walk with Jesus and influence others. Understanding how to live a Spirit-filled life is most important in walking with God.

Who is the Holy Spirit?

The Holy Spirit sounds almost spooky, mystical, and confusing. He is seen by some as mysterious, perhaps an emotion, a feeling and weird cosmic force — so much so that we don't talk about him very much. However, the Holy Spirit is the most relevant person for you in your daily life.

The Holy Spirit is a person. He is the third person of the trinity: Father, Son, and Holy Spirit. Throughout the Bible, the Holy Spirit is translated as a helper, advocate, counselor, and comforter. Below are verses describing the Holy Spirit:

> *And I will ask the Father, and he will give you another Counselor to be with you forever-- the Spirit of truth* (John 14:16).

> *But the Counselor, the Holy Spirit, whom the Father will send in my name, will teach you all things, and will remind you of everything I have said to you* (John 14:26).

> *But when he, the Spirit of truth, comes, he will guide you into all truth. He will not speak on his own; he will only speak what he hears, and he will tell you what is yet to come* (John 16:13).

The Bible teaches that the Holy Spirit is a person who permanently lives in us. The Holy Spirit has also been translated as "Friend." I recently read a book titled, *Union with Christ: The Way to Know and Enjoy God*. In this book, author

Rankin Wilbourne writes of the Holy Spirit saying, "The only thing that could be better than having Jesus with you, beside you, would be having Jesus within you, wherever you are and wherever you go" (page 50). The Holy Spirit is a person, our friend, who is always with us.

Why did the Holy Spirit come?

It's important to understand why the Holy Spirit came to earth. Just as Jesus had a very specific reason to come to earth (to die for the sins of the world and give us an opportunity to know and walk with him), so, too, the Holy Spirit has a very specific purpose. There are several tremendously beneficial reasons the Holy Spirit came.

1. To guide us in truth. As stated in John 16:13, the Holy Spirit came to help point us to truth, to walk with God, and to help us discern.

2. To help us experience all God wants for us. *Now we have received not the spirit of the world, but the Spirit who is from God, that we might understand the things freely given us by God* (1 Corinthians 2:12, ESV).

3. To help us experience intimacy and depth in our relationship with God. *But the fruit of the Spirit is love, joy, peace, patience, kindness, goodness, faithfulness, gentleness and self-control* (Galatians 5:22-23).

4. To experience a new life with God through Jesus Christ, God's love and the assurance of being a daughter or son of God. *For you did not receive a Spirit that makes you a slave again to fear, but you received the Spirit of sonship. And by him*

we cry, *"Abba, Father." The Spirit himself testifies with our spirit that we are God's children* (Romans 8:15).

5. To comfort and to counsel. As stated in John 14:26, *the Holy Spirit came to provide us with counsel. He also came to comfort, advocate, and strengthen.*

6. To help us live a life pleasing to God. *But I say, walk by the Spirit, and you will not gratify the desires of the flesh. If we live by the Spirit, let us also keep in step with the Spirit* (Galatians 5:16, 25, ESV).

7. To give us power. In Acts 1:8, immediately before Jesus ascends to heaven, he turns to his followers and says, *"But you will receive power when the Holy Spirit comes upon you; and you will be my witnesses in Jerusalem, and in all Judea and Samaria, and to the end of the earth"* (ESV). The Holy Spirit came to give us power to share our story with others, and power to live the Christian life.

How are we filled with the Holy Spirit?

Jesus promises to quench our thirst and satisfy our deepest needs and desires. In John 7:37-38, he says, *"If anyone thirsts, let him come to me and drink. Whoever believes in me, as the Scriptures has said, 'Out of his heart will flow rivers of living water'"* (ESV).

How exactly can Jesus quench our thirst? What does he mean? Right after Jesus says this, we read, *Now this he said about the Spirit, whom those who believed in him were to receive, for as yet the Spirit had not been given, because Jesus was not yet glorified* (John 7:39, ESV).

A person receives the Holy Spirit after becoming a follower

of Jesus. In other words, when you asked Jesus to come into your life, God sent his Holy Spirit to reside in you. To live in you. To abide in you. However, this does not mean the Holy Spirit is always controlling (filling) you. To be filled with the Holy Spirit, to be controlled by the Holy Spirit in our daily lives is something we simply ask for.

Spiritual Breathing

Christians fall short like anyone. Romans 3:23 says *all fall short of the glory of God.* Sometimes this seems to be especially true of me! One day on our way home from church, I snapped at one of my children. My tone of voice, my words, everything about how I communicated with my son was wrong. I was not feeling well; anything seemed to annoy me on this day (I know, I am such a good Christian), and I just wanted to be alone. Being alone when you have four children and are driving a minivan is very difficult. I know this because I have had much practice in this area.

When I mess up like this, whether it feels big or small, I practice something called spiritual breathing. I learned about spiritual breathing when I was in college, and to this day, I practice it when I fall short in my thoughts, words, and actions. Spiritual breathing is a very tangible practice that helps me get right with God and helps me depend on him.

Breathe Out: As soon as I realize I have sinned, I confess it. Confessing sin involves repentance (turning from my sin and going the opposite direction), and a change in my attitude and action. 1 John 1:9 says, *If we confess our sins, he is faithful and just and will forgive us our sins and purify us from all* *unrighteousness*. When I sinned against my son that day after church, I confessed my sin to him (I told him I was sorry and asked him to please forgive me) and to God, and I thanked God for forgiving me.

Breathe In: Ask God to fill you, to empower you, and then surrender control of your life (thoughts, words, and actions) to Christ. As you are filled with the Spirit, you will live in a way that makes God happy. *But those who are controlled by the Holy Spirit think about things that please the Spirit* (Romans 8:5b, NLT). The Bible promises that the Holy Spirit will then control you with his presence. 1 John 5:14-15 says, *This is the confidence we have in approaching God: that if we ask anything according to his will, he hears us. And if we know that he hears us— whatever we ask—we know that we have what we asked of him.*

I remember hearing about how to be filled with the Holy Spirit for the first time. I learned how God wants to experience intimacy with me. He wants to use me to help others. He wants to grow his fruits in my life. Again, the fruits of the Holy Spirit, according to Galatians 5:22-23 are, *love, joy, peace, patience, kindness, goodness, faithfulness, gentleness, and self-control.* I remember reading this and thinking, "Wow, I want to live a life that is defined by these fruits. I want God to produce these fruits in my life."

Do you want God to produce these fruits in your life? Do you want to live a life that is directed and empowered by God? To do so, we simply ask God to fill us, to empower us with the Holy Spirit by faith. By faith (belief), we will experience the power and fruits of the Holy Spirit. *I pray that out of his glorious riches he may strengthen you with power through his Spirit in your inner being, so that Christ may dwell in your hearts through faith* (Ephesians 3:16-17).

Being filled with the Holy Spirit is done through faith. An obvious way to express this faith to God is through prayer. In a previous chapter, we defined prayer as simply talking with God. Below is a suggested prayer to be filled with the Holy Spirit.

> *God, I confess to you that I often sin against you and try to control my life. Thank you for always forgiving me of my sins. Thank you for loving me and sending Christ to die for my sins. I invite Christ to sit on the throne of my life. Fill me, control me, with your Holy Spirit. I pray this in the name of your son Jesus. Thank you for filling me with the Holy Spirit and for directing my life. Amen.*

Does this prayer express the desire of your heart right now? If so, pray at this moment and trust God to fill you with his Holy Spirit, and to produce the fruits of love, joy, peace, patience, kindness, goodness, faithfulness, gentleness, and self-control.

A Better Understanding

It's important to have clarity in our relationship with the Holy Spirit. It's important to remember that when we become Christians, the Holy Spirit comes and lives inside of us. However, just because the Holy Spirit lives inside of us does not mean the Holy Spirit always controls us. Below are three analogies I share with people when teaching about the Spirit-filled life:

1. **Getting Drunk** - Ephesians 5:18 says, *Do not get drunk*

with wine, which leads to debauchery. Instead, be filled with the Spirit. Why would the author of this passage, the Apostle Paul, choose alcohol when explaining the importance of being filled with the Holy Spirit? Consider these similarities:

- Control: When drunk, a person is controlled by alcohol. When a person is filled with the Holy Spirit, they are controlled by God.

- Joy: People often drink looking for joy. However, alcohol is just a cheap counterfeit or substitution for real joy that is available to us from God. Joy is a fruit given to us when we are controlled by the Holy Spirit (Galatians 5:22-23).

- Love: When drunk a person is freer with their affections and emotions. When controlled by the Holy Spirit, a person has a higher capacity to love.

- Comfort: People often turn to alcohol for comfort in times of grief or depression. The Holy Spirit is referred to as the "great Comforter."

- Boldness in Speech: Boldness sometimes characterizes someone who is drunk; often, it's embarrassing. When a person is filled with the Holy Spirit, they are bold in proclaiming the Gospel, what they believe is true about Jesus, and how God has changed their lives (Acts 1:8).

2. **Dancing** - Galatians 5:25 says, *Since we live by the Spirit, let us keep in step with the Spirit.* I would rather be chased out of the ocean by a shark than dance (okay, maybe that's an exaggeration), so I don't relate much to this analogy. The Holy Spirit leads us as we keep in step "with him." As we live our lives filled with the Holy Spirit, we move

in step with him. We are in harmony with his wishes and our lives become more satisfying and fulfilling.

3. **Chocolate Milk** - The Holy Spirit comes to live inside us when we experience salvation. *And you also were included in Christ when you heard the message of truth, the gospel of your salvation. When you believed, you were marked in him with a seal, the promised Holy Spirit* (Ephesians 1:13). My friend, Roger Hershey, often says that being filled with the Holy Spirit is like pouring chocolate syrup into a glass of milk. The syrup is there at the bottom of the glass. When you shake it up, the milk is transformed into looking like the chocolate. Similarly, when we are filled with the Holy Spirit, we are transformed.

Surf Like Toledo

One of the best surfers in the world today is young Filipe Toledo. A passionate Brazilian, Toledo has competed on the World Championship Tour since 2013, and is known as one of the sport's most progressive, innovative, and powerful surfers. Toledo dominated the World Qualifying Series (just below the World Championship Tour), won several tour events, and continually posts perfect 10s in his heats. The world knows that there is no question if Filipe Toledo will win a world title; the question is when and how many world titles will he win. Do yourself a favor and watch the YouTube clip of Toledo at Jeffrey's Bay; you will be inspired!

I recently read an interview with Toledo that captures much of what we looked at in this chapter. Filipe says that when he is surfing, he tries to take what the wave gives him without forcing things to happen. Of course, he can, at times, plan out what he performs on the canvas of the wave: the cutbacks, the tubes, the off-the-lips, and other maneuvers. However, he only does what the wave allows him to do. Again, he allows the power of the wave to control his surfing.

As Christians, we are all given the power of the Holy Spirit - the fundamental concept that helps us walk with Jesus.

Most of us have not been given the ability to surf like Filipe Toledo. However, as Christians, we are all given the power of the Holy Spirit - the fundamental concept that helps us walk with Jesus. As we are filled with the Holy Spirit, we will grow as Christians who are known by the fruit of their lives. Walking with God throughout life is not about trying to be a better person, "working hard" or "having life together." Now, if we could only surf like Filipe Toledo!

Questions for
Personal or Group Reflection

1. Who is the Holy Spirit and why do you want to be filled by him?

2. What are the fruits of the Spirit?

3. What is spiritual breathing and how can this help you?

4. Who should be in control? And why?

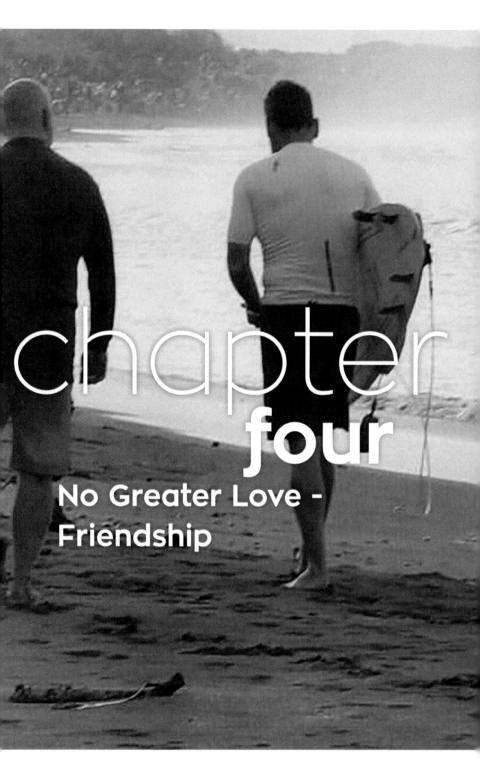

chapter
four

No Greater Love -
Friendship

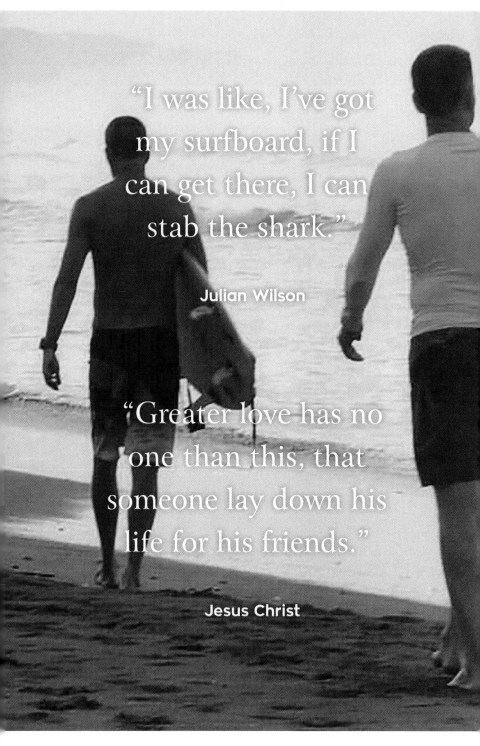

"I was like, I've got my surfboard, if I can get there, I can stab the shark."

Julian Wilson

"Greater love has no one than this, that someone lay down his life for his friends."

Jesus Christ

On July 19, 2015, I woke to no less than a dozen text messages on my phone. "Shane, did you see the Fanning/Wilson heat?" "Are you watching this?" "I can't believe Fanning is okay." With my heart beating a mile a minute, I jumped online to see what was happening.

I couldn't believe it. Right there, with the world watching, one of my favorite professional surfers from Australia had been attacked by a great white shark.

Australia is known for its incredible waves, beaches, and surfing. I've visited Australia several times. I've had the privilege of surfing its eastern coast. I'm always left admiring the culture and the people (and the fish and chips are amazing). Two of my favorite Australian surfers are Mick Fanning and Julian Wilson.

Fanning is a surfing legend, having won three world titles and numerous surfing competitions around the world. Julian Wilson is younger than Fanning, has yet to win a world championship, and is expected to take the mantle of Australian surfing royalty now that Fanning has retired. Both of these surfers are known as world-class athletes who are also good friends.

At a World Surf League (WSL) competition in South Africa, both Wilson and Fanning had surfed their way into the finals. It was an amazing display of surfing and both surfers blitzed their way to the final heat against one another. As the horn rang, signaling the beginning of the final, Julian Wilson caught a wave and rode it all the way down the point. As Fanning looked for his first wave, the unthinkable happened—he was attacked by a great white shark.

The scene, though lasting only thirty seconds, felt like a lifetime as I watched it over and over (accounting for only some of its 30 million views on YouTube). Fanning is thrown off his surfboard, disappears underwater, emerges a few seconds later, and is punched in the face by the shark's tail. As a wave approaches, Fanning is seen swimming without his surfboard, helplessly treading water, with the world wondering when the shark would bring him down again.

Miraculously, Fanning's life was spared. Personal watercraft rushed to the scene and pulled both him and Wilson from the water. The final was canceled and the athletes agreed to split the prize money and championship points.

What captivates me more than anything about this story is how Julian Wilson reacted when Fanning was attacked. I have a picture of how Wilson responds when Fanning is dragged underwater. In the middle of the chaos, Wilson paddles straight toward the shark.

Yes, you read that correctly. Wilson did not panic and paddle away from the shark. He paddled toward it.

What would you do if you saw a great white attack someone a hundred or so yards out to sea? How would you respond?

Think about it.

Instead of thinking of how he would get to safety, Wilson rushes to the danger of deeper water. He literally swam toward his friend, whom he thought almost certainly was going to die, to try to help him. A reporter asked Wilson what he was thinking. Through tears, Julian answered the reporter, "I thought I might be able to stab the shark with my surfboard."

Wilson was literally willing to give his life for his friend.

Friendship in the Bible

The life of Jesus is marked by relationship. Jesus constantly spent time with his friends, teaching them, serving them, encouraging them, and loving them. In the book of John, verse 15:13, Jesus speaks of friendship when he says, *"This is my commandment, that you love one another as I have loved you. Greater love has no one than this, that someone lay down his life for his friends"* (ESV).

Proverbs 18:24 says, *A man of many companions may come to ruin, but there is a friend who sticks closer than a brother.* Ecclesiastes 4:9 says, *Two are better than one, because they have a good reward for their toil* (ESV). One of my favorite friendships in the Bible is between two women, Ruth and Naomi, whose friendship defines loyalty and sacrifice: "Where you die I will die, and there will I be buried. May the Lord do so to me and more also if anything but death parts me from you" (Ruth 1:17, ESV).

My best friend is my wife, Laura. Laura is an amazing woman and a gift to my children and me. One of my favorite memories of our friendship is the evening I asked her to marry me.

We drove to a small town outside of San Diego (La Jolla) to have dinner. We walked down the hill to a small and secluded cove and sat down to watch the sunset. I do remember the waves looked quite fun (sometimes surfers have one-track minds), but I mostly remember my heart beating so hard I thought it would come out of my chest!

La Jolla is a popular place for scuba divers and this evening was no different. I pointed out to Laura someone surfacing from a dive about fifty yards in front of us in the water. We watched as this diver, covered in a wetsuit, hood, snorkel, tank, and mask, swam toward us. He crawled ashore, pulled off his swim fins, took the breathing tube from his mouth, and walked straight up to Laura.

"Excuse me, is your name Laura Powell?"

Laura had no idea how to respond. With a confused look she said that yes, she was indeed Laura Powell. The scuba diver said, "Oh good, because I believe this belongs to you. I just found it at the bottom of the ocean."

He pulled a large conch shell from a webbed sack attached to his back, handed it to Laura, and walked up the beach.

We were both freaking out.

I asked Laura to look inside the shell. She nervously opened it and found a diamond ring. I took the ring, got on my knee, looked her in the eyes, and asked if she would please, please, please, be my wife. Fortunately, she said yes, and Laura and I have been married for twenty-three years.

As we prepared for the wedding, we went to pre-marital counseling with our pastor. During these sessions, we learned what to expect after we tied the knot, and how to prepare to live with each other for the rest of our lives. There was one word we heard over and over from our pastor: communication.

All relationships, whether it's with a spouse, a parent, a surfing buddy, or teammate, are built on communication. It's vital in every relationship. This is true in a relationship with God and this is true in our relationships with friends. Below are four principles of communication that have helped me walk in my relationship with God and with my friends.

Fellowship

"Go, Shane! Stop thinking and just paddle! You got it!" I put my head down, paddled as hard as I could, and threw myself over the ledge of one of the bigger waves I surfed that week in Nicaragua. Sheer luck determined that I would not fall. I dropped a good twelve feet to the bottom of the wave, bottom turned into the pocket, and stood tall while the wave exploded behind me.

With adrenaline surging, I kicked out a few hundred yards down the line, looked up at my friend Brent, and waved. I had Brent to thank for that wave. Without his encouragement, I never would have dropped in.

Brent has been a close friend for years. We met at UC Santa Barbara as we led a small group Bible Study in the dorms on campus. When we would meet to plan these Bible studies, we would do so in the Pacific Ocean while surfing. A "board meeting," if you will.

Our friendship has grown over the years. My relationship with Brent is based on our mutual love for God, but it is also centered quite a bit around our love for surfing. We have surfed various waves in Southern and Central California, Mexico, Latin America, and Puerto Rico. As we have traveled and surfed together, our friendship has grown.

This idea of being together and bonding over shared interests is what the Bible calls fellowship. In Acts 2:42, Jesus' good friend Luke says, *"And they devoted themselves to the apostles' teaching and the fellowship, to the breaking of bread and the prayers"* (ESV). The early Christians spent time together—they were in fellowship—and, as a result, the church grew.

This idea of being together and bonding over shared interests is what the Bible calls fellowship.

Hebrews 10:24-25 says, *And let us consider how to stir up one another to love and good works, not neglecting to meet together, as is the habit of some, but encouraging one another, and all the more as you see the day drawing near* (ESV). Fellowship is important, as it brings us encouragement and spiritual strength. Think of a campfire. Just as logs burn more brightly when placed together, so Christians need each other for warmth and encouragement.

Dr. Bill Bright, the founder of Cru, the organization I work for, said this about the importance of fellowship: "The Greek word for fellowship, *koinonia*, means sharing in common. We desperately need to share our Christian experience with others who love God and walk with Him, and likewise allow them to share with us. The church, where we can meet other Christians and hear God's Word, is God's appointed place for Christians to meet. Bible studies and meetings on campus are also extremely helpful."

Prayer

Several years ago, my wife and I made a decision to move from Southern California to Puerto Rico, and then, two years later, to Florida. These were the hardest decisions we have ever made. Our families and friends are in Southern California. We have history in Southern California. We love the surfing, the culture, the food, the weather, and the many things to do as a family. On top of all this, our kids were settled in a great school and had never really known a different home than Oceanside.

For over twenty-five years, I surfed Oceanside Harbor. The Harbor is a special place for me. I took guys in my Bible study surfing there when I was in college. My wife and I lived there when we were first married. I baptized my children in its waves. My family and I, including my sisters and my extended family, have many memories on this stretch of beach and ocean.

When people ask how Laura and I decided to move from a place we love, we always answer with one word: prayer. After much prayer together and by ourselves, God was clear that it was time for our family to move.

The north end of the Oceanside Harbor has a long jetty that stretched several hundred yards into the Pacific Ocean. For much of my life, I have connected with God through "prayer walks" along this jetty. As I would walk, I would talk to God. I thanked God for the many blessings he had given me. I asked God for guidance in my marriage, family, and career. I prayed from the book of Psalms, asking God to help in times of depression, conflict, trials, and decisions.

Prayer is simply talking with God. From beginning to end, the Bible speaks of prayer. God desires to grow in a relationship with us, and prayer is key in growing in that relationship. Jesus speaks much of and lives out the importance of prayer. As I have studied his life, I see three main areas where Jesus focuses:

1. **Jesus prayed with his friends.** Talking with God,

thanking God, asking God for guidance and wisdom, is also meant to be communal at times. There are many examples in the Bible where we see Jesus gathering his friends to pray. *Now about eight days after these sayings he took with him Peter and John and James and went up on the mountain to prayer* - Luke 9:28 (ESV).

2. **Jesus prayed alone.** Of course, prayer is something that can be very personal, private, and intimate. The life of Jesus is also marked by times with God by himself, as evidenced in Luke 5:15-16: *But now even more the report about him went abroad, and great crowds gathered to hear him and to be healed of their infirmities. But he would withdraw to desolate places and pray* (ESV).

3. **Jesus prayed often.** Prayer is not reserved only for Sundays, when we need something, or are feeling desperate—though God does want to hear from us then, too. Prayer is to be done all throughout our days, regardless of circumstances. Jesus models this in Luke 6:12: *In these days he went out to the mountain to pray, and all night he continued in prayer to God* (ESV). The apostle Paul says in 1 Thessalonians 5:16-18 to pray often: *Rejoice always, pray without ceasing, give thanks in all circumstances; for this is the will of God in Christ Jesus for you* (ESV). We are to pray when we want something as we read in Mark 11:24: *Therefore I tell you, whatever you ask in prayer, believe that you have received it, and it will be yours. And we are to pray when we are feeling stressed and anxious, Do not be anxious about anything, but in everything by prayer and supplication with thanksgiving let your requests be made known to God.* (Philippians 4:6-7, ESV).

How can you grow in your friendship with God and others? Pray. Pray together. Pray alone. Pray often. More on this will be written in a later chapter, but prayer is so key in our friendships, I wanted to mention it here as well.

Service

Anyone who reads about the life and lasting influence of Jesus Christ will agree he is one of the greatest leaders to ever live. His teachings have changed lives, families, communities, and nations. Even though he lived over 2,000 years ago (on the other side of the world from most of us), his life and leadership left a legacy all over the world.

Jesus turned leadership upside down when he taught. When Jesus walked the earth in first-century Palestine, power was key and authority was at a premium. The best way for the Romans to use their power and leadership was to march through the streets of Jerusalem with mighty horses and centurions, always willing and ready to physically enforce their will, which they did often. Leadership was all about power, position, and prestige.

So when Jesus taught on leadership as recorded in Mark 10:43-44, he no doubt turned some heads by saying, *"But it shall not be so among you. But whoever would be great among you must be your servant, and whoever would be first among you must be slave of all"* (ESV).

Jesus teaches that to lead and influence means to serve and bless. In Luke 9:48, he says, *"For he who is least among you all is the one who is great"* (ESV).

Last year on a surf trip to Central America, my friends and I woke up early to check the waves. After pouring some amazing

Costa Rican coffee, we wandered down to the beach to see exactly what the surf was doing. After about 15 minutes of watching some really good-looking sets pour in, we ran back to our room to wax our surfboards and load up on sunscreen.

As we approached our room, I remember looking at my friend Pete and asking him with a hopeful tone, "What's the smell... is that bacon?!" (Everyone loves bacon, especially when you are burning calories on a surf trip.) As we entered our casita, we stepped into a feast: bacon and eggs, fruit, toast, juice, and, of course, more fresh Costa Rican coffee.

Our friend Phil had stayed behind and made us breakfast. It tasted so good that I found myself comparing it to Thanksgiving dinner!

When I think of friends who have influenced me to do good for others, to make a difference in people's lives, to encourage others, and to grow in my relationship with God, very few people compare to Phil. Phil has led me through being a servant in so many ways over so many years. Through his servant's heart, Phil has brought me closer to Jesus.

John Stott is an English author and leader who once said, "Leaders have power, but power is safe only in the hands of those who humble themselves to serve." Another well-known author, Oswald Sanders, wrote, "True greatness, true leadership, is achieved not by reducing men to one's service but in giving oneself in selfless service to them" (Spiritual Leadership, Moody Press).

To grow in a relationship with God and our friends means we are to serve them. Jesus teaches that to serve means to lead. When my good friend Phil has served me (and so many others over the years), he has led me closer in my relationship with God and we have become even better friends.

Bible Study

My family and I recently lived in Puerto Rico. Puerto Rico is a beautiful island and happens to have some pretty good surfing, too.

The winter season brings strong swells from the North Atlantic Ocean. These swells travel unhindered to the north and west sides of the island. Something unique about "la Isla Encantada" is that the second-deepest underwater trench in the world sits right off its northern coast. This means nothing slows down the marching of big surf. This, as a surfer knows, produces much stoke. :)

On extra-large wave days, when the surf is too big for most of the island, a reef comes to life in the coastal town of Aguadilla. Waves reel into the bay, usually groomed by offshore winds, and will break for several hundred yards to shore.

Towards the end of our first winter there, an especially large eight- to twelve-foot northwest swell was lighting up the coast. My oldest son and I paddled out on one of these days. The conditions were right out of a dream: sunny, very light winds, warm and tropical water, and long rides to shore. However, I had one problem that I was not yet aware of: my leash was weak and would not stand the pressure of these larger waves.

My son and I had an amazing surf session. As the sun went down, I kept saying what every surfer says when they need to go in to the beach, "Just one more good wave. Then I'll go in. It's so good out here, just one more..." Well, after saying that four or five times, I knew I really needed to get going! I spotted a solid set wave, paddled deep, and dropped in one of my biggest waves that day.

As I stood and raced down the line, I bottom-turned into the pocket (the most critical part of the wave). Unfortunately, another surfer was caught out of position and I had to turn to avoid him. Avoiding running this poor guy over meant the wave crashed on the back of my surfboard, throwing me head first into the Caribbean Sea and pushing me a good ten feet down into the reef. After feeling like I was in a washing machine for far too long, I surfaced to notice my leash had broken.

I watched helplessly as my surfboard was pushed into the rocks on shore, breaking the fins, and dinging it beyond repair.

A surfboard leash keeps the surfer connected to the surfboard. If my leash had not broken, my surfboard would have remained connected to me. If my leash had not broken, my surfboard would not have been smashed on the rocks. If my leash had not broken, I would have avoided a 400-yard swim to shore!

Like a leash to a surfboard, the Bible keeps us connected to God and to one another. The Bible is a book of rock-solid wisdom that addresses how we can grow in our relationships. Studying the Bible, especially with others, is key in growing in our relationship with God and our friends.

In Luke 10:25-27, an attorney asked Jesus a question for which we would all like an answer: *And behold, a lawyer stood up to put him to the test, saying, "Teacher, what shall I do to inherit eternal life?" He said to him, "What is written in the Law? How do you read it?" And he answered, "You shall love the Lord your God with all your heart and with all your soul and with all your strength and with all your mind, and your neighbor as yourself"* (ESV).

How can we grow in our understanding of God and have eternal life? How can we love God with all our hearts, souls, strength, and mind? How do we best love our neighbor? Read, study, and memorize the word of God.

In my final year as an undergraduate, I realized I needed one more science course to fulfill the graduation requirements of UC Irvine. I really did not want to mess with my morning surf schedule, so I took a Botany course that met from 11-11:50 a.m. on Mondays, Wednesdays, and Fridays.

It seemed that most Mondays, Wednesdays, and Fridays had very good waves, and I missed that Botany course quite a few times the first half of that academic quarter. The uncrowded and consistent waves were too hard to deny. I mean, how much will it really matter if I didn't study or go to class that often?

It mattered quite a bit, actually.

When I took the mid-term exam halfway into the quarter, I knew little of the material. I failed that test and I failed it in spectacular fashion. I did not know how to respond to the problems in front of me, as I had not studied. How could I know the answers if I had not prepared?

I was a man on a mission the second half of that course. After much personal study and group study with my fellow Botany classmates, I received an A- on the final, barely getting a C for my final grade. Here's my point: When I was not committed to studying and learning the material, I stumbled when I took the test, and I failed miserably.

The more I studied about plants by myself and with my classmates, the better I did on the test. This principle is true in the Christian life. If I am reading, meditating, memorizing, and studying the word of God, I grow in my understanding of how God wants me to live my life. I still fail at times, but the miracle of God's grace and forgiveness covers my many shortcomings (more on this miracle in our last chapter).

SUIJ - Surfers Under the Influence of Jesus

Jesus ate often with his friends. Fellowship, conversation, and enjoyment of one another were done much of the time over good food.

When I was a youth pastor in Southern California, I would meet with several other guys to go surf and, of course, to eat. This group turned into a weekly time with our college group from church when we would spend hours together trading waves, eating tacos and burritos, and studying the Bible together.

Each Friday morning, we would check the waves in Del Mar, Solana Beach, or Cardiff Reef and paddle out together. After wearing ourselves out in the Pacific, we would meet up at the world famous, at least world famous in my mind, Potato Shack. The Potato Shack is a well-known breakfast and lunch local restaurant in Encinitas, California. Even as I type this, my mouth is salivating—the egg burrito is out of this world and is what we will eat in heaven.

All of a sudden I am very hungry.

We called ourselves SUIJ (pronounced sewage): Surfers Under the Influence of Jesus. We loved coming together to surf and to eat each Friday morning. As we fellowshipped on the water and over food, we spent time praying together, studying the Bible together, and serving together at church. The result of these times was a strengthening in our relationships with one another and in our relationship with God. I learned much about friendship from those men.

Twenty-five years later, I am still in touch with some of the guys from SUIJ. One of them, my friend Robert, even hand-shaped for me a surfboard last summer.

Now I'm going to go make an egg burrito. :)

Questions for
Personal or Group Reflection

1. Prayer, service, fellowship, and Bible study are all ways we can grow in our friendship with God and others. How can you apply these to your life right now?

2. Who in your life has modeled being a servant to you? How can you learn from them?

3. In the book of Luke, Jesus says, *"You shall love the Lord your God with all your heart and with all your soul and with all your strength and with all your mind, and love your neighbor as yourself."* How do you think Jesus defines the word "neighbor"?

4. Who is your neighbor? How can you love your neighbor as yourself?

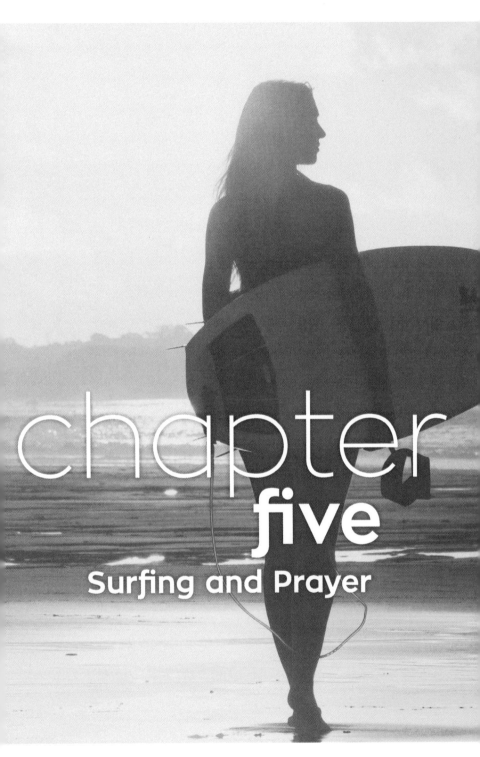

chapter
five
Surfing and Prayer

"Surfing can be a
religious experience"

Tom Curren

Three-time World Surfing Champion

February 18, 2002 started like any other day off for me. A friend and I were planning a drive up north to check a fickle right-hand point break, the air was a perfect seventy-five degrees, there was a solid four to six foot northwest swell hitting the coast, and the water was an uncharacteristically warm sixty degrees. It was going to be an uneventful and relaxing day of surfing.

The day was hardly relaxing and it was hardly uneventful.

As I poked around my garage deciding which surfboard to ride, my wife came in and said she was not feeling well. She had been up even earlier than me with an upset stomach. The catch here is that she was seven months pregnant with our twins. Her pregnancy was considered "high risk" as twins are often delivered early. We realized it would be a good idea to go to the hospital and check to make sure Laura and the babies were okay.

No less than ten minutes after walking into the hospital, the doctor looked at us and said in no uncertain terms, "Laura, you're dehydrated and your babies are in distress. You are going to deliver these twins today."

We were shocked and not expecting to hear that.

I looked at our doctor and said, "Wait...today?"

The doctor turned to me and said emphatically, "Yes, Shane. Today. Actually, in about ten minutes. We will begin an emergency cesarean section now."

She wasn't kidding. Within ten minutes, an army of doctors, nurses, and machines were surrounding my wife to ensure a successful delivery of my son David and daughter Summer. A C-Section happens quickly. The doctor made an incision below my wife's stomach, opened things up, and pulled both babies out of her. It really was amazing.

What concerned the medical staff was my son David's umbilical cord. I watched the doctor straining to unwind the cord that was coiled three times around his neck. David's skin was a blue color, he was not breathing well, and a nurse rushed him to the neonatal intensive care unit.

As the nurse ran my son to another part of the hospital (I'll never forget his little feet sticking out of a blanket), I said the words, "God, please protect my son."

We often pray in times of crisis. We also pray in times of celebration and hope. We pray out loud, in our hearts, before meals, in large groups, and by ourselves.

What exactly is prayer and how can it help in our lives? Why should we pray and what exactly does it look like in our daily lives?

This chapter will attempt to answer these questions as we see how prayer is a chief means in helping us grow in our relationship with God and why prayer is so important in the Christian life.

What is prayer?

Prayer is simply talking with God, conversing with God, communing with God. Every follower of Jesus has a direct line of communication to God that is always available to us. Over the years of growing as a Christian, I have learned that prayer is so much more than words or an activity. Prayer is more of an experience and ongoing conversation in a loving relationship.

A main way I grow in my relationship with my wife is to

converse, to listen, to communicate (and even after twenty-three years of marriage, I have a long way to go here). This is a critical way we grow as friends and as husband and wife. Likewise, it is critical we talk with God and listen to him, in order to grow in our relationship.

Prayer is simple. As we pray, we are telling our father what we desire and trust that he will do what is best. Jesus speaks of this in Matthew 7:7-11:

> *Ask, and it will be given to you; seek, and you will find; knock, and it will be opened to you. For everyone who asks receives, and the one who seeks finds, and to the one who knocks it will be opened. Or which one of you, if his son asks him for bread, will give him a stone? Or if he asks for a fish, will give him a serpent? If you then, who are evil, know how to give good gifts to your children, how much more will your Father who is in heaven give good things to those who ask him! (ESV)*

But prayer is also difficult. Our minds wander as we may not fully understand prayer. We have many questions about prayer that makes praying challenging for us. Why does God answer some of our prayers and not others? How do we know if God is listening? How many times do we need to pray to make a difference? These are just a few questions that may discourage us from praying.

In order to better understand prayer, let's first look at why we should pray.

Why should we pray?

Prayer helps us against temptation

Several years ago, I was on a surf trip with a good friend. After several hours of trading waves with locals and my buddy, I took one last wave to the beach. I walked up the trail and watched the sun begin to set while I waited for my friend to finish his surf session. As I sat down, another visiting surfer approached me. I introduced myself and we began to have a conversation about surfing, our travels looking for waves, and our families.

After a few minutes, and as he rolled a joint of marijuana, he asked if I'd like to smoke with him. I remember thinking, "I'm a thousand miles from home and my friend will be in the water for at least another 30 minutes. No one would ever know."

God understands temptation. Jesus was tempted throughout his life and specifically prays to God to help him overcome it. In the twenty-second chapter of Luke verse 40, Jesus says, *And when he came to the place, he said to them, "Pray that you may not enter into temptation."* Other writers throughout the Bible speak of overcoming temptation. In 1 Corinthians 10:13, Paul writes of God's faithfulness when we are tempted: *No temptation has overtaken you that is not common to man. God is faithful, and he will not let you be tempted beyond your ability, but with the temptation he will also provide the way of escape, that you may be able to endure it* (ESV). When we are in a moment of temptation, which is often, ask God to help you to escape it. This is a prayer God will answer.

When my new friend offered me his marijuana, I prayed under my breath, "God, help me to handle this well and in a way that honors you." I then looked at him, thanked him for the offer, and politely declined. He said, "No problem," and we spoke for another thirty minutes while watching the surfers. When you are tempted, pray and God will answer you.

I want to make an important note here. When we fall into temptation, whatever the circumstance, remember God's infinite love, grace, and forgiveness. As I write in other places through this book, it's vital we remember how God views us even when we fall short. Have you fallen into temptation recently? I know I have. If so, ask God's forgiveness and help in resisting the next time you are facing temptation.

Prayer helps us know God's will

Life is full of decisions. I recently purchased a new surfboard. I kept asking myself questions about the details of my new board. Should I order a longer board this year? One with more volume and thickness, or one that is narrower? What about the fin options? It really is amazing the amount of decisions made when ordering a surfboard!

God is definitely concerned with the details of our lives. However, he is more concerned with our hearts and who we are becoming and less so with our day to day decisions. I have always believed when we speak of God's will we are looking at the bigger picture of his desires in our lives. This bigger picture is about our character, our salvation, and our relationships.

Prayer is crucial as we seek God's will, God's desires. An entire chapter in this book is devoted to understanding and determining the will of God, but it is also important to mention here. 1 John 5:14 says, *And this is the confidence that we have toward him, that if we ask anything according to his will he hears us* (ESV). This verse tells us to ask. Asking is praying. If we ask according to God's will, he will hear us.

And then in Colossians 1:9, we read of a leader praying for his friends to know God's will: *For this reason also, since the day we heard of it, we have not ceased to pray for you and to ask that you may be filled with the knowledge of His will in all spiritual wisdom and understanding* (NASB). It is important to pray not just for ourselves in knowing God's will, but that others will know God's will also.

Prayer helps us grow in our relationship with God

This is the best reason to pray: to grow in our personal relationship with the creator of the universe. One of the unique things about Christianity is that it is not a religion based on a set of rules. There is no other religion, worldview, or philosophy that is based on grace. All others are based on rules and standards. Christianity is not about standards, duty, or doing things to make us right with God. Christianity is about a relationship.

Yes, it is important for us to live to higher standards. As we grow in our relationship with God, as we get to know him better, we become better followers of him. God and Jesus have standards, but not standards that make us right with them. We become Christians through grace - it is a grace relationship.

One of the best ways we grow in this grace relationship is through prayer.

I love what Ephesians 3:14-19 says as Paul prays for his friends:

> *For this reason I bow my knees before the Father, from whom every family in heaven and on earth is named, that according to the riches of his glory he may grant you to be*

strengthened with power through his Spirit in your inner being, so that Christ may dwell in your hearts through faith—that you, being rooted and grounded in love, may have strength to comprehend with all the saints what is the breadth and length and height and depth, and to know the love of Christ that surpasses knowledge, that you may be filled with all the fullness of God (ESV).

Paul prays that his friends would experience an intimate and closeness "of Christ." This intimacy is what drives us to pray. Prayer is not just an exercise designed to make God see and do things our way. Prayer is our means of growing in an intimate relationship with Him. This intimacy is what God wants with us. We read this in James 4:8: *Draw near to God, and he will draw near to you* (ESV).

Prayer helps God's work grow

Working as a minister around the world has given me the opportunity to see people do amazing things for God. On one particular campus, our college students wanted to help their peers hear more about how Jesus impacted and changed their lives. They organized what came to be known as the "I Agree with Glenn" week.

On a Monday morning, all of the students at UC Santa Barbara wore bright orange t-shirts that said "I Agree with Glenn" in bold letters. "I Agree with Glenn" was plastered on posters throughout campus, written on chalkboards in every classroom; there were even advertisements taken out in the school newspaper and on the bus that drove though campus. At the bottom of each advertisement was an invitation to come to a meeting on Thursday evening where people could come and hear from Glenn.

Glenn was a junior at UC Santa Barbara. His life had been changed by Jesus Christ a few years earlier. Glenn was going to simply tell his story and share how others could know and grow in a relationship with God.

Over 800 students came to hear from Glenn that evening. I remember a student saying, "All week, I've been wondering who Glenn is and what exactly all of you people agree about." Glenn shared his story and another student shared as well. The meeting ended with thirty-five students indicating that they, too, wanted to receive Christ and know God personally. We spent the rest of that year meeting with students who came to that meeting, helping them understand God's love for them.

Students not involved in planning that week did not see the incredible amount of prayer that went into "I Agree with Glenn." Our students prayed for big things. Students prayed for God to work on the campus of UC Santa Barbara in bold ways. Students prayed for God to show up and change lives. Students prayed for Glenn as he boldly shared with his peers how important his faith is to him.

And God showed up. I believe the success and fruit of that week was the result of students praying.

Prayer gets things done. God has chosen to live his life and do his work through us, and much of this happens through prayer. The Bible is full of stories of God's people praying and God responding.

Prayer is important to God

Perhaps this reason is the most obvious: we pray because it

is important to God. The Bible in its entirety is full of prayers. Jesus was constantly praying throughout his life, as recorded in the Gospels. The Apostle Paul speaks of prayer over forty times in his writing and there are over 650 prayers throughout the Bible (with over 450 recorded answers to prayer). God commands prayer, tells us how to posture ourselves in prayer (more on this later in this chapter), what to pray for, who to pray for, and why we should pray.

A leader I have worked with, Dan Hayes, in his article about prayer, says that we should pray because it's so valuable to God. "In many ways, it is the most compelling, if only because it is not linked to any sort of earthly result. It is this: prayer itself is inherently valuable to God. In other words, whether we ever see any answers (and we will) and whether we ever derive any personal benefit (and we will), God views prayer standing alone with an incomprehensible value."

How should we pray?

We've defined prayer as simply talking with God and being in a conversational relationship with him. We've also looked into why we should pray. But how do we pray? What does prayer practically and tangibly look like in our lives?

Prayer is a lifestyle, something we can do without even thinking about it. Yes, there are times when we are very intentional in connecting with God, but a life of prayer is a life of living in God's presence. One of my favorite authors is the late pastor Henri Nouwen. In one of his books on prayer, he speaks to this:

Prayer is a lifestyle, something we can do without even thinking about it.

"To walk in the presence of the Lord means to move forward in life in such a way that all our desires, thoughts, and actions, are constantly guided by him. When we walk in the Lord's presence, everything we see, hear, touch, or taste reminds us of him. This is what is meant by a prayerful life. It is not a life in which we say many prayers, but a life in which nothing, absolutely nothing, is done, said, or understood independently of him who is the origin and purpose of our existence" (Page 28).

To live this life of prayer and be in the presence of God day in and day out, there are several practices I aim to consistently live out. By simply practicing these prayer disciplines, I learn to better communicate with God and our relationship grows. As my pastor recently told me, "We learn to pray by praying."

1. **Set a consistent time each day to converse with God.** One of the first things I do each day is check the surf. There are numerous websites that will tell us what the waves are like, the forecast for the rest of the day and the week, and when it is best to paddle out. However, even before I look at the waves on the internet, I spend some time reading my Bible and praying. Jesus prayed early as we see in Mark 1:35: *And rising very early in the*

morning, while it was still dark, he departed and went out to a desolate place, and there he prayed (ESV). Each day I pray for wisdom in the various facets of my life. *If any of you lacks wisdom, let him ask God, who gives generously to all without reproach, and it will be given him* (James 1:5, ESV). You may be asking, "What exactly do I pray?" A great model of prayer is given by Jesus himself in Matthew 6:9-13: *Pray then like this: "Our Father in heaven, hallowed be your name. Your kingdom come, your will be done, on earth as it is in heaven. Give us this day our daily bread, and forgive us our debts, as we also have forgiven our debtors. And lead us not into temptation, but deliver us from evil"* (ESV).

2. **Pray throughout the day.** The Psalmist prays throughout the day: *Seven times a day I praise you* (Psalm 119:164). 1 Thessalonians 5:17 says to pray without ceasing. As I pray throughout my day, I share with God my concerns, worries, and anxieties. God wants to hear us from and gives us peace as the Bible says, *do not be anxious about anything, but in everything by prayer and supplication with thanksgiving let your requests be made known to God. And the peace of God, which surpasses all understanding, will guard your hearts and your minds in Christ Jesus* (Philippians 4:6-7, ESV). By praying at all times in the Spirit, with all prayer and supplication. *To that end keep alert with all perseverance, making supplication for all the saints* (Ephesians 6:18, ESV). My son and I pray together before each heat in our various surfing competitions. I pray with my kids as we drive to school or go on errands together. We pray before our meals. God wants us to communicate with him throughout our days.

3. **Prayer Walking and Prayer Paddling** - Surfing is an excellent time to talk with God. I will paddle for several

hundred yards and pray while doing so, especially when I am alone. Of course, when a wave comes to me, I will drop in and surf it, then paddle back while I am praying out loud. There is something that helps me connect with God by praying, and even singing, out loud while I am in the ocean. When I am not in the ocean, I like to prayer walk. I walk my neighborhood, the campus I work, or wherever in the world I am (with my travel schedule, I mean that quite literally). Prayer walking and prayer paddling is also a great way to get some exercise while connecting with God.

4. **Follow the WAVE Model of Prayer** - When I pray, as I paddle and walk, early in the morning with my cup of coffee, or throughout the day, I often follow the WAVE model of conversing with God.

Worship - Worshiping God reminds us of who he is and of his love and care for us. Jesus modeled this in his teaching about prayer in Matthew 6:9: *Pray then like this: "Our Father in heaven, hallowed be your name"*(ESV). When I am using the WAVE model of prayer, I simply say things like, "God, you are all-knowing, you are gracious, you are loving, and you are kind. God, you are so good, you are beautiful, you are gracious and merciful."

Admit your Sin - The A in the WAVE model of prayer stands for admission. It's important to confess our sins and ask forgiveness. This reconnects us in our fellowship with God. Our relationship with God is unchanged by sin, but our fellowship is damaged. Fellowship is a word that is defined by sharing, being in community with, and partaking together. For example, if I yell at my daughter and use an unkind word toward her, our relationship remains unchanged. I am still her father and she is still my daughter. However, our fellowship is damaged. To be in right fellowship with her, I admit my sin to her and ask forgiveness. When I sin toward God, I simply say, "God, you know where I have failed you. Please forgive me for my selfishness, for the way I spoke to my children or wife, for my impure thoughts..." The Bible clearly says in 1 John 1:9, *If we confess our sins, he is faithful and just to forgive us our sins and to cleanse us from all unrighteousness* (ESV). Admitting our sin brings us back into right fellowship with God.

Voice Gratitude - The V in WAVE stands for voice your gratitude. Psalm 118:1 says, *Give thanks to the LORD, for he is good; his love endures forever.* The Bible says that every good and perfect thing comes from God, and I use this time to thank him for the many good things he has given me. I thank God for my wife and children, my parents and sisters, for the opportunity I have to breathe each day, the gift of life, the gift of surfing, and so much more! On a way home from surfing in Cocoa Beach recently, my son looked at me and said, "Dad, thanks so much for taking me; I appreciate it." I loved hearing gratitude from my son. God loves to hear gratitude from his children as well.

Earnestly Ask - You may find this hard to believe, but God wants to hear what we want from him. Recently, I read a birthday wish list from one of my boys. As I looked at his list, I smiled. I loved what I was reading. No, he would likely not receive all he was asking - and it was quite a long list - but as his father, I want what was appropriate for him. Jesus speaks to this when he says, *Ask, and it will be given to you; seek, and you will find; knock, and it will be opened to you. For everyone who asks receives, and the one who seeks finds, and to the one who knocks it will be opened. Or which one of you, if his son asks him for bread, will give him a stone? Or if he asks for a fish, will give him a serpent? If you then, who are evil, know how to give good gifts to your children, how* *much more will your Father who is in heaven give good things to those who ask him!* (Matthew 7:7-11, ESV)

During this time of prayer, I ask God for wisdom in parenting and decision making, I pray for my children, for our leaders, and other things going in my life at the time. Yes, I do at times pray for surf!

"God, please protect my son."

I prayed those words at least one hundred times over the next several hours. David's lungs were undeveloped, so the doctors put him into neonatal intensive care. His twin sister, Summer, also had health concerns and was placed with David. For the next eight days, Laura and I watched as nurses drew blood to test their oxygen levels, continuously fed intravenous tubes into their tiny veins, and changed an unbelievable amount of diapers. Throughout this time, I drank several gallons of coffee a day (or more), visited Laura as she healed from her surgery, and spent time with my two-year-old daughter getting the house ready for two newborns.

What I remember most from that season of life is how much I prayed. I prayed on my knees at various times of the day. Laura and I prayed together over Summer and David in the intensive care unit. I prayed with nurses, my pastor prayed with and for me, and my friends prayed with me. Lots of praying!

Summer and David are no longer four pound preemies. Summer dances for The Orlando Ballet Company and School and David recently placed 3rd in the Eastern Surfing Association Regional Championships. I think it's fair to say their lungs are no longer undeveloped.

Questions for
Personal or Group Reflection

1. What is prayer?

2. Why should we pray?

3. What is the WAVE model of prayer?

chapter
six

Mexican Jails and Understanding God's Will for Your Life

Surfer pictured: Shane Sebastian

"There is more than one right way to ride a wave."

Jamie O'Brien

Professional Free Surfer

My first big decision as a young adult was deciding where I would attend college. Growing up in Southern California, I wanted to stay somewhere close to home but go away at the same time. I applied to several universities and ended up deciding between two schools that were, of course, near the ocean: The University of California Irvine and The University of California Los Angeles.

Everyone had an opinion about where I should attend school, but even after several months of research, I was unsure. So, one morning I tossed my surfboard into my Hyundai hatchback, jumped on the 405 Freeway, and drove to check out both UC Irvine and UCLA.

I decided I would visit UCLA first. As I passed through Orange County and headed past Huntington Beach, Long Beach, and eventually to Westwood (near UCLA), the traffic continued to slow. Everything you have ever heard about traffic in Southern California and Los Angeles is painfully true—it's horrible! There are just too many people and cars in one place, so it's often more of a parking lot than a freeway.

When I arrived at UCLA, I could not find a place to park. I drove around and around with no success. Thirty minutes later, I gave up. Out of frustration, I decided I would drive to the beach and go surfing, then come back for a campus tour later.

At the beach, I again couldn't find parking. Ugh! On top of there being no parking spots, there were no waves. This was not how I thought the day would go for me. I drove back to the UCLA campus and still could not find a place to park. This was getting ridiculous. As I swore under my breath (yes, I was not exactly Christ-like in the moment) and almost began to pull my hair out, I found the onramp for the 405 South and decided to look at UC Irvine.

Forty-five minutes later, I pulled into a large parking spot on the campus of UC Irvine—without even looking for one. The campus was quiet and beautiful. I walked around a large park in the middle of campus and ended up crossing a bridge to what could quite possibly be what we will eat for lunch in heaven: In and Out Burger!

I then drove to Newport Beach, not far from campus, and went surfing. The waves were incredible; I surfed three to five-foot waves with only a few other people in the water. As the sun set over the Pacific Ocean, I thought more of where God wanted me to go to college. I knew where I wanted to go to college, but was it where God wanted me to go to college?

My friend, Claude Hickman, author and the U.S. Director of the non-profit organization The Traveling Team, challenges

---

God is not so much telling us
what to do in every decision,
but pointing us to abide.

---

people with the simple idea that God calls people into a shared life with him. There is not always a specific path God wants us to take. Hickman speaks of the importance of obeying God. God is not so much telling us what to do in every decision, but pointing us to abide. God gives us a compass, not a map, to live our lives.

God is more interested in our hearts than in the details of our lives. I remember a friend of mine who was struggling about a particular job opportunity. He was offered a role in a company that seemed like a good fit, but he was agonizing over if it was exactly what God wanted. I remember asking him, "If you are seeking God, walking with him, don't you think he is okay with whether you say yes or no to this job?" My friend was growing in his relationship with God, so my suggestion to him was to simply keep doing what he was doing and take the job. I helped him understand that God wanted to continue to live in a trusting relationship together; that was most important.

God gives us the general direction. The Bible is a relational book that helps us grow in a friendship with him. God is most concerned with how we are following him; the rest of life should follow this relationship.

For example, a student in my Bible study was dating a woman who he thought he wanted to marry. He asked me how to know if it was God's will to marry her. I asked him, "Do you think God has just one person out of seven billion on this planet that you will marry? If so, how do you know she is the exact one?"

I went on to share with him that God wants us to walk with him, follow his commands in the Bible (of which there are many concerning dating and marriage), and go from there. This student had been dating for over a year, he and his girlfriend were both walking with God, and they did marry within the year.

A Surf Trip and a Mexican Jail

Life is constantly bringing us decisions. Some are big and some are small. As I shared in an earlier chapter, my family and I made a big decision to move from our home in Southern California to Puerto Rico a few years ago to work with college students for two years. I've had many friends ask me how I knew that was the right decision.

Do you ever make a decision and then think, "Was that the right call? How do I know it's really what God wants?" Do you ever feel nervous about or second-guess your decisions? How do we rest in our decisions? I rest in those decisions by reminding myself that God is always present, always near, even in my doubts and fears.

I remember a particular surf trip to Mexico with my best friend way back in college. The waves were excellent on that trip, but what I remember most was being pulled over by the Mexican police. This was normal and happened often on our surf trips.

The way it would normally play out is we'd ask what the problem was, listen to the police bring up several false and ridiculous charges of speeding or littering, and then offer to pay them $30 cash. That number would normally double, and then we would be on our way across the border.

Not this time.

My friend Jim was in no mood to negotiate, even though he had left shotgun shells in his truck from a previous hunting trip. The cops were not happy about those shells. But Jim said he would pay no fine, after which the cops said they would take us to the jail for processing.

I was getting nervous.

Jim looked at the cops and simply said, "Okay, let's do that. Good idea, guys. Let's go to the jail. In fact, I'm a friend of the police chief. We built houses together here in Rosarito last summer. Let's go see him and see what he has to say."

Because Jim knew the police chief, we were allowed to get back in the truck and drive across the border. The police looked at me and said, "You can go, too; you're with him." I was with Jim, so I had nothing to worry about.

All over the Bible, we see a God who is always with us, always present in the big and small decisions. In the Old Testament, God calls Jeremiah to be a prophet to the nations, not just to the nation of Judah but to the nations. A big job. How does Jeremiah respond? This soon-to-be great leader responds with fear, anxiety, and excuses.

Their interaction goes like this:

God: "Jeremiah, before I formed you I knew you, and before you were born, I consecrated you; I appointed you a prophet to the nations. I am calling you to be a leader."

Jeremiah: "Lord God, I do not know how to speak, for I am only a youth. I really don't know what to do."

God: "I am with you, Jeremiah. I am always with you."

The rest of the story tells us that Jeremiah does obey God. And he was no doubt encouraged, knowing that God would be with him as he followed the Lord's will. God was with him, so he had nothing to worry about.

The God spoken of in Jeremiah is the same God we speak of—and hear from—today. No matter what decision you make as you live out God's will, remember God's never-ending presence in your life. Remember that, as you think about the small and big decisions in life and you pursue the will of God.

As I've worked with students and young people from all over the world, I've noticed three ways they approach God's will: the conventional approach, the confusing approach, and the calling approach.

Let me briefly explain these.

The Conventional Approach: Give Me a Detailed Blueprint!

Many of us are infatuated with the idea that we must have a very detailed and specific call from God as we make decisions, especially the bigger decisions. God can, at times, speak to us very specifically when he calls us to do something, as we see with Jeremiah in the example above. In my experience, however, this does not happen very often. When we wait for God to tell us exactly what to do, we create a problem.

My previous pastor in Southern California, Larry Osborne, writes of the problem this way: "There's no cosmic Easter egg hunt required to see who can find God's will and who gets left with an empty basket. But, unfortunately, that's how many of us feel. The problem stems from a concept many of us have been taught from birth. We've been led to believe that God has a highly detailed blueprint for our life that includes a specific, preordained job, career, house, spouse, car—and everything in between. As a result, we spend a lot of time looking for that special person, place, or thing that we think God has set aside just for us. It's the egg we hunt for."

A blueprint is very specific and very detailed and must

be followed precisely or the overall plan will be at risk. My brother-in-law is an architect and my father is a developer. My brother-in-law draws up highly detailed plans, then passes the blueprint on to my father, the builder. My father follows the details of the blueprint. If my father fails to follow even a small detail of the blueprint, the whole project can fall apart.

Unfortunately, this is how many people approach discernment of God's will for their lives. They want a detailed blueprint. You don't always need a detailed blueprint!

Why should we avoid this conventional approach to God's will? First, the implication that God's will is a detailed blueprint for one to follow implies that a single wrong turn can make everything collapse. Friends, please understand that God is, indeed, concerned with what we do. Of course he is. But God is much more concerned with who we are than with dictating our lives.

God has a plan for you—not a blueprint. His plan is that you walk with him and become like his son Jesus as you live

---

God has a plan for you— not a blueprint.

---

day to day. I think young people—all people—feel freedom when they hear this. As Micah 6:8 states, *He has shown you, O mortal, what is good. And what does the Lord require of you? To act justly and to love mercy and to walk humbly with your God.* Or as St. Augustine said: "Love God and do what you desire." In other words, it is the quality of one's heart and intention that are most important to God. Don't skip over this truth: God is most concerned with who we are, not what we do.

God will likely call you to go to certain places, to do certain things for him, to take a certain role or position, to live in a certain place. We see God call people to specific things throughout the Bible. However, God first and foremost calls us to follow and be like him.

As the apostle Paul writes in Romans 12:2: *Do not conform any longer to the pattern of this world, but be transformed by the renewing of your mind. Then you will be able to test and approve what God's will is—his good, pleasing, and perfect will.* God's will is not about a detailed blueprint; it is about renewing our minds.

The Confusing Approach: Just Show Me What You Want!

The conventional approach to knowing God's will is just one we gravitate to. We can also follow a much more mysterious approach, what I refer to as "the confusing approach" to knowing the will of God. I recently had a student say to me, "I just wish God would show me what he wants!" It was spoken as if God's desires were hidden. God's will is not a mystery to unravel; there is nothing hidden about God's will for you. As Pastor Kevin DeYoung writes, "God's will is not an unexplained labyrinth whose center we are supposed to discover."

God's will has to do with the things we already know. We don't always know exactly how things will turn out. However, the Bible outlines several things that are God's will. Below are four things God wills for you:

1. God's will is that we have a relationship with him.

The apostle Paul wrote to a young pastor and friend of his named Timothy: *God desires all people to be saved and to come to the knowledge of the truth* (1 Timothy 2:4, ESV). 2 Peter 3:9 speaks of God's will that everyone knows him: *The Lord is not slow to fulfill his promise as some count slowness, but is patient toward you, not wishing that any should perish, but that all should reach repentance* (ESV). Jesus speaks of God's love for every person when he says in John 3:16: *For God so loved the world, that he gave his only Son, that whoever believes in him should not perish but have eternal life* (ESV).

God's will is first that you enter into a personal relationship with him. This is what God created you for. As we grow in our relationship with him, we understand his desires for us as his children. As author Dr. Dallas Willard said, "A coworker sees what needs to be done and simply does it. We become so close to God that we do not have to wait to hear his words. We don't have to be asked."

2. God's will is that we be filled and controlled with the Holy Spirit.

The Bible speaks often of God's desire for us to be filled, to be empowered by his Holy Spirit: *Therefore do not be foolish, but understand what the will of the Lord is. And do not get drunk with wine, for that is debauchery, but be filled with the Spirit* (Ephesians 5:17-18, ESV). To the church in Galatia, the apostle Paul writes, *But if you are led by the Spirit, you are not under the law* (Galatians 5:18). Scripture is clear that if we want wisdom to know God's will, we must be Spirit-filled. As we are filled with and directed by the Holy Spirit, we will know what God desires for us. Something to remember is that as a Christian who believes in Christ, you are guided by the Holy Spirit and you can trust your decisions. And as we grow closer to God through his word and Spirit, we will know God's will!

Something I find interesting is that the Old Testament speaks much more specifically to people about what God actually wants them to do. God tells Moses to lead the Israelites. God tells Jeremiah to lead his nation. God tells Jonah to warn Nineveh. He speaks to his people clearly.

In the New Testament, instead of telling his followers more of what he wants them to do, God tells them more of who he wants them to follow and become. This happens after God has sent his Holy Spirit to live inside of his followers in the book of Acts. As I've come to understand this, I am more compelled to walk with God and be empowered by him.

3. God's will is that we be set apart to be used by him.

All over God's word, we read about his desire for us to become more and more like him. 1 Thessalonians 4:3 says, *For this is the will of God, your sanctification* (ESV). Hebrews 10:10 says, *And by that will we have been sanctified through the offering of the body of Jesus Christ once for all* (ESV). To be sanctified means to be set apart, to be made holy for God's use. This fancy word simply means to become more like Jesus. Our role as we live our lives is not so much to find something, but to become someone more like the person of Jesus.

I remember a good friend of mine calling me after Christmas one year. A large storm was brewing up near the Aleutian Islands near Alaska. These powerful winter storms blow strong winds that send large waves to the coast of California and Mexico. He and I looked at The Weather Channel (The Weather Channel is a surfer's favorite television channel) and decided to go on the hunt for some big surf.

As I prepared for the trip, I dusted off my very special surfboard for larger waves—what surfers call a "rhino chaser" or big wave "gun." A year earlier, my surfboard shaper had made me this very special tool for big waves.

In the Old Testament, we see God using special tools in the temple to bring him glory. The Bible says these tools are set apart to be used in a way that will bring God honor and praise. Then in the New Testament, God uses the same word to describe his people, to describe us! We, too, are set apart to be used to bring God honor and praise.

Do you believe this? Ask yourself that question right now: "Do I believe that God has set me apart to walk with him and influence others?" Believe it, friends. God has set you apart

---

God has set you apart to influence and to bless others, to help others experience a relationship with him.

---

to influence and to bless others, to help others experience a relationship with him.

4. God's will is that we do what we want.

This sounds almost unspiritual, doesn't it? Yet, this has a

very strong theological foundation. Live a life obedient to God and go from there. Walk with Jesus and see where God leads you. Abide and seek him in life and he will direct you.

See what Paul says about this in Philippians 2:12-13: *Therefore, my beloved, as you have always obeyed, so now, not only as in my presence but much more in my absence, work out your own salvation with fear and trembling, for it is God who works in you, both to his will and to work for his good pleasure* (ESV).

As God works in our lives and as we submit to the guidance of the Holy Spirit and to the process of sanctification, God motivates and guides us to make decisions that are in line with his will. As one author writes, "The biblical doctrine of providence suggests that God works within the redeemed believer to form desires which accord with his will." In other words, God will make his desires your desires as you grow in your relationship with him.

The most common question asked of me as a minister and missionary is: How do I know God's will for my future? Young people (most people, to be honest) are confused and derailed as they "try to figure out" what God wants them to do in the area of missions and in their lives in general. The reminder here is that God wants you to walk with him in whatever decision you make.

I want to help people understand that as they practice right intentions and grow in Christlikeness, they can trust God to guide them throughout their lives. It's important to state the obvious here. The four steps above are not meant to model a program that, if properly followed, will result in knowing every aspect of God's will. The will of God in the life of a Christian is to be the result of a growing relationship. The steps above merely point to the aspects of that relationship.

The Calling Approach: "I'm Waiting for God to Tell Me"

"No aspect of Christian mission is more puzzling than this problem of a call." - J. Herbert Kane

In my conversations with students about their future, the most common concern or excuse is, "But I'm not sure if God has called me there." It's as if one needs a special revelation when making decisions. I refer to this as the "calling" approach to finding the will of God.

I heard a pastor once say, "There is a general obligation resting upon Christians to see that the Gospel of Jesus Christ is preached to the world. You and I need no special call to

---

You don't need a special calling from God to live—you simply obey God and move forward.

---

apply that general call of God to our lives." A general calling is already there. This also addresses what some call the "Lightning Bolt Calling Myth." This myth suggests that people must have a miraculous calling experience when making significant decisions. You don't need a special calling from God to live— you simply obey God and move forward.

God calls all of us to live a life that is pleasing to him. It really is that simple. Walk with God and make decisions as they come. One of my favorite authors is Kevin DeYoung.

Pastor DeYoung writes in his book, *Just Do Something*, "The question God cares about most is not 'Where should I live?' but 'Do I love the Lord with all my heart?'"

As you walk with him, become more Christ-like, and do what he wants, God will use you in ways that will expand his kingdom and change the lives of people you meet. I believe God especially does this with young people!

God's Will for my College Experience: UC Irvine or UCLA?

After several hours of fun waves and as the sun set over the Pacific Ocean, I thought to myself, "Well, that was an easy decision. I am going to be a college student at UC Irvine." I drove home that night and told my parents I would be attending The University of California in Irvine. I loved being an Anteater (UC Irvine's mascot). The friends I made, my spiritual growth, and the academics were a gift to me in that season of my life. Oh, and the surfing was excellent, too.

How did I decide where I would spend my college years? Surfing, In and Out Burger, a parking spot, and traffic. Okay, perhaps that is simplifying it a bit! However, I really do believe God was giving me a few options and then telling me to go where I wanted. I sensed God saying to me, "Shane, walk with me and then decide on where you want to go. Whatever you decide, continue to walk with me."

Yes, knowing God's will can be that simple.

Questions for
Personal or Group Reflection

1. Look again at the three ways many people view calling. How have you typically viewed calling: The conventional, the confusing, or the calling approach?

2. Have you ever thought that God's will is that we do what we want? Explain this in your own words.

3. How would you respond to someone if they asked you right now, "How do I determine God's will for my life?"

4. What challenges you most about knowing God's will?

chapter
seven

Locals Only

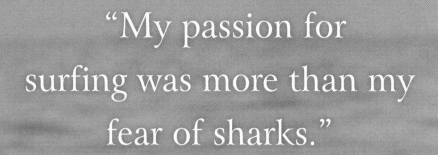

"My passion for surfing was more than my fear of sharks."

Bethany Hamilton

"Do not fear, for I am with you."

Jesus

Bethany Hamilton is a Kauai native who began her surfing career at the young age of 11. By age 13, she was an accomplished surfer and well-respected in the surfing world. Hamilton came to international attention after her left arm was bitten off by a tiger shark while surfing on October 31, 2003. Several weeks later, Bethany was back on a surfboard and has since made a full recovery. She has made a mark surfing big waves. She has even returned to competitive surfing. In 2016, Hamilton finished in 3rd placed in the World Surfing League's Fiji Pro. In large open ocean conditions, Hamilton surfed her way to the semi-finals against the best in the world....with one arm.

In her book, *Soul Surfer*, Hamilton speaks of her relationship with God, "When I was about five, I gave my heart to Jesus Christ and since then, it's just been a stronghold in my life. Really, through the shark attack and all the hard times that my family and I went through, it gave us unity and perseverance to push through all this crazy stuff that we never knew was going to happen." Bethany Hamilton has shared her story all over the world and as a result, many have come to faith in Jesus Christ.

Right before Jesus ascends to heaven, he gives these words to his followers, *Therefore go and make disciples of all nations, baptizing them in the name of the Father and of the Son and of the Holy Spirit* (Matthew 28:19). Jesus asks his followers to tell others about him. This is God's plan to help the world know about him. Hamilton has taken this very seriously, and views her life as an opportunity to share God's love with others. Do we see our own lives as opportunities to share God's love with others? How exactly do we do that?

Over the past 25 years, I have had the opportunity to teach others how to share their faith, to help them learn how to tell their story, and be a part of pointing others to Jesus. The most common reason people do not share this story is simple: fear. Common questions asked to me as I train people are: What if I offend someone? What if I don't know how to answer a specific question? How do I actually start a conversation with a friend about what it means to begin a relationship with God?

To address our fears in sharing our story with others and point them to Jesus, we need to look at three main components.

1. What does it mean to share our faith?
2. Why should we share our faith?
3. How should we share our faith?

What does it mean to share our faith?

I remember a particular small group Bible study in a dorm at UC Santa Barbara. I was sitting on a bunkbed with a group of freshmen students spread throughout the room. We were looking at a fascinating story in the book of Acts. In Acts 8:34 we read, *And the eunuch said to Philip, "About whom, I ask you, does the prophet say this, about himself or about someone else?"* (ESV) Philip, a follower of Jesus, was able to speak to a very influential African about Jesus. The story results in this African becoming a Christian, who was likely one of the first followers of Jesus Christ on the continent.

I explained to these students that this is an early example of a Christian sharing their faith. This didn't seem to resonate with my students, so I used two words to help illustrate my point: witness and ambassador.

The word witness simply defines someone who explains what

they have seen and experienced. They testify to what they believe is the truth. The apostle Paul speaks of this in Acts 20:24: *But I do not account my life of any value nor as precious to myself, if only I may finish my course and the ministry that I received from the Lord Jesus, to testify to the gospel of the grace of God* (ESV).

In a court of law, an eyewitness is called to testify to what they have seen, what they have heard, and what they have experienced. God calls us to do the same. As you share your faith, you are being a witness.

We are witnesses and we are also ambassadors. Paul speaks of the idea of being an ambassador in 2 Corinthians 5:17-20: *Therefore, if anyone is in Christ, he is a new creation. The old has passed away; behold, the new has come. All this is from God, who through Christ reconciled us to himself and gave us the ministry of reconciliation; that is, in Christ God was reconciling the world to himself, not counting their trespasses against them, and entrusting to us the message of reconciliation. Therefore, we are ambassadors for Christ, God making his appeal through us. We implore you on behalf of Christ, be reconciled to God* (ESV).

To share our faith simply means to share our experience in knowing God (witness), and to represent our home (ambassador).

An ambassador is one who is appointed to represent their country in a foreign land, one who is a ranking government representative stationed in a foreign capital. Our ultimate home is heaven. As ambassadors of our ultimate home, we are called to help others reconcile (become right) with God. One of the cornerstones of foreign diplomatic missions, and a privilege for any ambassador, is to work for peace. As ambassadors we help people find peace with God. To share our faith simply means to share our experience in knowing God (witness), and to represent our home (ambassador).

Why Do We Share Our Faith?

Santa Barbara, California, is a special place. The people, the mountains running into the ocean, the incredible Mexican food, the climate and culture make this small seaside town a real gem. Living in Santa Barbara for over ten years, I have experienced its beautiful attributes, as well as some of its incredible beaches. There are waves in parts of Santa Barbara county that God took much pride in creating!

The curse of Santa Barbara surfing is the Channel Islands ten miles off its coastline. These islands block all south swells that would otherwise pour into Santa Barbara seven or eight months of the year. So, surfers wait eagerly - and impatiently - for strong northwest swells to march down offshore past Washington, Oregon, and, ultimately, peel into the many nooks and crannies along the coast.

One year, during one of these anticipated northwest swell events, my neighbor and I drove to a secret spot just north of our home. We parked behind a large tree on Highway 101, loaded up our backpacks with our wetsuits, booties and other necessary items, grabbed our surfboards, and started our hike to the coast. A mile or so later, we looked out at empty six-foot, glassy, perfect surf. We rushed to put our wetsuits and booties on, scrambled down the cliffs faster than mountain goats, and surfed blissfully for three hours.

On our hike back to the car, we spoke of our incredible surf session. We were full of stoke as we relived each wave - we could not believe how lucky we were to surf by ourselves. However, this stoke didn't last long as we heard a voice from behind us, "Hey, you kooks (a kook is a negative term for someone who pretends they are a surfer)! Who the —— are you? What the —— do you think you are doing here?" A middle-aged man, with a very large stick, was walking toward us. In no uncertain terms, he was telling us that he did not appreciate our surfing at "his" spot.

The beach we surfed was very private and few people knew how to get there. Because of this, not many people surfed the waves when it was good. Though this wave was on a public beach, this old guy with a big stick was threatening us to keep it quiet, "You guys better keep this secret!" He was clear that he did not want to see us ever again at "his surf spot."

This bullying tactic is known as localism. Localism manifests itself through both verbal and physical abuse to keep people away from surfing a particular surfing area. Unfortunately, I have seen or first-hand experienced localism all over the world. Whether it's at a crowded wave in Southern California or Hawaii, a remote beach in El Salvador or Puerto Rico, or a reef pass only accessible by boat in the South Pacific, I have seen surfers threaten and even physically assault someone for being at "their" spot.

The point of these locals is to keep their wave a secret. They want no one to know of the beauty and stoke the particular wave can bring.

In Christianity, we want to live the opposite as the local guy

I met surfing that day - we want to tell anyone and everyone of the beauty and stoke of the Christian life. Christianity should never be secret.

Christianity should never be secret.

Why are we to be witnesses and ambassadors? Too many reasons to count! Let me share the top reasons of why I am motivated to share the good news of Jesus with others:

1. God has given a clear command to every Christian.

God's plan to bring people into a relationship with him is through his people. Right before Jesus ascends to heaven and forty days after his resurrection, he gathers his followers on a hill outside of Jerusalem. Jesus looks at those who have come to trust him (this crowd likely consisted of no more than one hundred people) and tells them to go out and be witnesses to not just their friends and family, but to the world. In Acts 1:8 Jesus says, *"But you will receive power when the Holy Spirit has come upon you, and you will be my witnesses in Jerusalem and in all Judea and Samaria, and to the end of the earth"* (ESV).

Then in In Mark 16:15 Jesus says, *And he said to them, "Go into all the world and proclaim the gospel to the whole creation"* (ESV). And in Luke 24:46-48 Jesus says, *"Thus it is written, that the Christ should suffer and on the third day rise from the dead, and that repentance and forgiveness of sins should be proclaimed in his name to all nations, beginning from Jerusalem. You are witnesses of these things"* (ESV).

The last words of Jesus recorded in Matthew is to go and make disciples (a disciple is someone who follows Jesus), to be witnesses, to tell the world how they can know him. As in the other passages, this was not merely a suggestion for his early followers or for leaders in the early church or for those who may have much knowledge about the Bible. When Jesus gives this command, he makes it clear it is for every man, woman, and child who profess faith in him.

2. Men and Women are lost without Jesus Christ.

I work for a Christian organization that works with young people on high school campuses and universities around the world. At times, I have the opportunity to travel to some amazing places, Japan included. Japan's population is less than 1% Christian. For context, there are more Christians in Southern California than there are in the entire country of Japan.

I've had the chance to train and coach our teams that serve as ministers in Tokyo. On one particular trip, I was staying in a suburb of Tokyo, Mitaka. I woke early the first day and went for a long walk before I was to meet with our team. I walked to Kichijogi Park, watched a group of elderly Japanese practice Tai Chi, and turned around to walk back to my hostel. After thirty minutes, I realized I had passed the hostel. Wait, had I actually walked passed it? Or had I taken a wrong turn? Wait, did I go too far or not far enough? I had no idea. I could not read the road signs, no one I spoke to could help me due to the language barrier, and on top of that, it was starting to rain.

I was very, very lost.

It took some time for me to realize that I did not know the way to my destination. Fortunately, and once I realized I was lost, I finally found a nice Japanese man who, in broken English, was able to show me the way. Once I knew the way, I made it back to my hostel and then to my meetings.

People need to be told the way. People will not know the way to God unless someone tells them. Sometimes, people don't know they are lost until someone shares with them how God loves them and desires to know them personally.

These verses help us know how we can find and experience a relationship with God. *Jesus said to him, "I am the way, and the truth, and the life. No one comes to the Father except through me* (John 14:6, ESV). *And there is salvation in no one else, for there is no other name under heaven given among men by which we must be saved* (Acts 4:12, ESV).

3. People are hungry to know God

When he saw the crowds, he had compassion on them, because they were harassed and helpless, like sheep without a shepherd (Matthew 9:36).

Everywhere I go in the world, I encounter people who are hungry for spiritual things. Sure, some people are cynical toward religion. But overall, people are open to discussing what it means to have a personal relationship with God.

One day, back when I was in college (a long, long time ago), I was at work and able to talk with my friend, Arturo, from Southern Mexico, about how he could experience a relationship with God through Jesus Christ. I worked in the kitchen with Arturo and we were usually the last ones to finish the shift.

After work, we would always sit on the back dock and talk. Arturo spoke very little English and I spoke very little Spanish, and in some ways, we helped each other learn the other's language that year. After a month or so, I really wanted to talk with Arturo about how God was real, how God had changed my life, and how Arturo could know God, too. I was able to read a presentation of the gospel in Spanish to Arturo and he became a Christian.

What I remember most from that relationship was how interested Arturo was in God and Jesus. I think you'd be surprised at how many friends and family you have who are interested in God.

4. As Christians we have the greatest gift imaginable.

What's the best gift you have ever received? Think back to an early Christmas or birthday. When I was twelve years old, I remember coming out of my room at six o'clock on Christmas morning (which felt very late for me as my parents wouldn't let me come out any earlier!). As I ran up the stairs to the family room, I saw my gift, a new surfboard in the corner by the Christmas tree. To say I felt stoked was an understatement.

In his letter to the church in Ephesus 2:8-10, Paul writes of God's free gift: *For by grace you have been saved through faith. And this is not your own doing; it is the gift of God, not a result of works, so that no one may boast. For we are his workmanship, created in Christ Jesus for good works, which God prepared beforehand, that we should walk in them* (ESV).

A gift is free; it is unearned. When I received the surfboard from my parents, I didn't have to work for it. I didn't have to do more chores around the house, take the dog on a few extra walks, or weed the front lawn (I hated that). The word grace, used in the verses above, means unmerited favor or free gift. We read of God's gift to us in John 3:16-17: *For God so loved the world, that he gave his only Son, that whoever believes in him should not perish but have eternal life. For God did not send his Son into the world to condemn the world, but in order that the world might be saved through him* (ESV).

Personally, this is my greatest motivation in sharing my faith with others. The gift of salvation is not something that can be achieved or earned or accomplished. It is something that can never be attained on our own; it is something that can only be done to us and for us.

When I received my surfboard for Christmas, I called my friends to tell them. I was excited and wanted to share the good news with everyone. As a follower of Jesus, I've received the gift of salvation, the greatest gift I will ever receive, and I want to share this gift with others.

5. We are motivated by God's love for us and others.

I've been surfing for over thirty years, my entire adult life. I remember being asked by a friend why I devote so much of my time (and vacations) to surfing, why I don't pick up golf or another sport, and even why I wrote this book. I answered by simply explaining that I am doing these things because I love to surf.

Our motives, why we do what we do, explain our actions. This applies to followers of Jesus Christ and answers why we share our faith with others. In 2 Corinthians 5:14-15 Paul says, *For the love of Christ controls us, because we have concluded this: that one has died for all, therefore all have died; and he died for all, that those who live might no longer live for themselves but for him who for their sake died and was raised.* (ESV)

God's love has changed us and blessed us, and we want others to experience this change and blessing. From the love for God, we are compelled to share this love with others. We read this in John 14:21 where Jesus says, *"Whoever has my commandments and keeps them, he it is who loves me. And he who loves me will be loved by my Father, and I will love him and manifest myself to him."*

How Do We Share Our Faith?

Now let's get practical. How do we do this? What does it actually look like to point people to a relationship with God? Here are five suggestions that have helped me as I seek to introduce others to Jesus Christ:

1. **Prayer** - The most effective and strategic way to share our faith is to pray for others. I love this passage in Colossians 4:2-6: *Continue steadfastly in prayer, being watchful in it with thanksgiving. At the same time, pray also for us, that God may open to us a door for the word, to declare the mystery of Christ, on account of which I am in prison— that I may make it clear, which is how I ought to speak. Walk in wisdom toward outsiders, making the best use of the time. Let your speech always be gracious, seasoned with salt, so that you may know how you ought to answer each person* (ESV).

When I was in college, I went to a small group Bible study that looked deeper into this passage. The author, the apostle Paul, is writing this letter from prison. He writes to his friends who attend a church in the city of Colossae. Paul is asking his friends if they would pray for him to be able to share his faith with his jailor. Again, Paul is in a prison cell, literally chained to a wall. If I were Paul, I would be asking my friends to pray that God would get me out of jail!

Not Paul. Paul is asking his friends to pray that he would have an opportunity to "declare the mystery of Christ" and to make the good news of Jesus clear to those who are imprisoning him. Paul asks very specifically that he would have an opportunity to share his faith.

When I was in junior high, I often went to the beach with my church youth group. I usually invited my friends to join me. One of those was my buddy, Sam. Sam and I would boogie-board, get ice cream, go to the beach Bible study, and then take the bus home together. We were good friends throughout junior high and eventually lost touch as we went to high school.

Throughout life, I have often thought of Sam. Though we were friends for only three or so years, I have fond memories of our relationship. Over the last several decades, I have prayed for Sam; very specifically, I have prayed that Sam would come to know God personally. When I first understood the passage above, I began to pray for Sam.

Several years ago, I found Sam on Facebook. I asked if we could meet for lunch to catch up when I was in town later that month. I remember when I saw him—it had been thirty years—he looked much the same (except he was now much taller than me!). After spending time catching up, I told him that I had prayed for him off and on throughout my life. I told him I hoped it didn't sound weird to him, but I had prayed that he would come to know God personally as I had early in life. I remember feeling nervous as I shared this with him.

After several minutes, Sam looked at me and said, "Shane,

you won't believe this, but two weeks ago, I had someone share with me how I can know God personally through Jesus. He shared with me what you are sharing with me right now. I became a Christian last Tuesday, and my wife and son and I are starting to attend church nearby."

Prayer is the key to sharing our faith with others. Right now, think of someone you know who does not know Jesus, who

---

Prayer is the key to sharing our faith with others.

---

you can share with, who needs to understand "the mystery of Christ." God will answer this prayer!

We can pray expectedly for our friends. In 1 Timothy 2:1-4, Paul writes of God's desire to know everyone. God's desire is that all people come into a relationship with him: *First of all, then, I urge that supplications, prayers, intercessions, and thanksgivings be made for all people, for kings and all who are in high positions, that we may lead a peaceful and quiet life, godly and dignified in every way. This is good, and it is pleasing in the sight of God our Savior, who desires all people to be saved and to come to the knowledge of the truth* (ESV).

As you pray for your friends and as you pray for opportunities to talk with them about God, you can do so expectantly. As we read above, God desires all people to be saved and come to knowledge of the truth. You can be the person who helps your friend understand truth!

2. **Ask Questions and Listen Well** - How often do you find yourself already formulating a response when someone else is speaking? So often, listening is the key to a productive conversation. This is true in sharing our faith. The Bible speaks much of the importance of listening well. James 1:19 says, *Know this, my beloved brothers: let every person be quick to hear, slow to speak, slow to anger* (ESV). King Solomon writes in Proverbs 10:19, *When words are many, transgression is not lacking, but whoever restrains his lips is prudent* (ESV).

A few key questions you can ask in sharing your faith:

- Do you consider yourself a religious person?

- What is your religious background?

- If a friend of yours were to ask you how one goes to heaven, what would you say?

- How does one come to know God personally?

These are simple questions that can help initiate a conversation about God and Jesus. To better learn how to facilitate conversations on faith, go to startingwithgod.com, Cru.org, godtools.com, etc.

3. **Know What to Say** - I was in Europe recently and met with students who have created a simple way to have a discussion about God. They wear a plastic bracelet with four symbols; a heart (representing God's love), a line (representing the separation between God and us), a cross (representing Jesus Christ), and a question mark (representing the question God asks of us). A student explained to me how they use these bracelets: "It's really easy, Shane; when someone asks what the symbols on the bracelet mean, we simply explain them."

The Heart - The heart represents God's love for us. The Bible tells us that God created everyone in his image and that he desires to have a personal relationship with us. Psalm 16:11 speaks of God's desire to be with us throughout life: *You make known to me the path of life; in your presence there is fullness of joy; at your right hand are pleasures forevermore* (ESV).

The Line - The line represents sin. Sin simply means imperfection and is what keeps us from God. The Bible teaches in Romans 3:23 that no one is perfect, all are born into sin, for all have sinned and fall short of the glory of God.

The Cross - The cross represents Jesus' sacrificial death on the cross for our sins. God reaches down to us though Jesus. 1 Peter 3:18 says, *For Christ also suffered once for sins, the righteous for the unrighteous, that he might bring us to God, being put to death in the flesh but made alive in the spirit* (ESV).

The ? - The question mark represents an opportunity. Do you believe that God loves you and wants to be in relationship with you? The decision is yours, if you want to open the door of your life to Jesus: *Behold, I stand at the door and knock. If anyone hears my voice and opens the door, I will come in to him and eat with him, and he with me* (Revelation 3:20, ESV).

To get your own bracelets and a booklet explaining how to use them, go to thefour.com

4. **Be Confident** - Sometimes we simply need to be reminded of who God is and what he has done for us. In Paul's letter to Timothy, we read of a young pastor (Timothy) who is being reminded by his teacher that we don't need to be ashamed of God's work in our lives and of how much God has done for us. This reminder brings c:ourage *Therefore do not be ashamed of the testimony about*

our Lord, nor of me his prisoner, but share in suffering for the gospel by the power of God, who saved us and called us to a holy calling, not because of our works but because of his own purpose and grace, which he gave us in Christ Jesus before the ages began (2 Timothy 1:8-9, ESV).

5. **Deepen Your Own Faith** - I have found that the more I am growing in my relationship with God, the more confident I am in sharing my faith with others. On a recent surf trip to Puerto Rico, I was telling someone about my wife, Laura. Because I am so intimately connected to Laura, because I know her so well, I am able to describe her easily. Talking about our relationship is natural and fun for me, as we have been in a deep and growing relationship for over twenty-four years. If I am spending regular time with God, reading the Bible, spending time in fellowship with other Christians, and praying, I am able to better describe Jesus to those around me. These verses from Joshua 1:8-9 speak of the importance of studying God's word: *This Book of the Law shall not depart from your mouth, but you shall meditate on it day and night, so that you may be careful to do according to all that is written in it. For then you will make your way prosperous, and then you will have good success. Have I not commanded you? Be strong and courageous. Do not be frightened, and do not be dismayed, for the LORD your God is with you wherever you go* (ESV).

6. **Use Various Websites and Resources** - A few of my favorites are startingwithgod.com, godtools.com, and Cru.org.

Key Definitions

There are times when I go surfing and I actually catch very few waves. I recently had a surfing session where I only caught three waves and I surfed them poorly. I was cold, my leash was continually entangled in my feet when I stood on my board, and no matter how hard I tried, I could not catch any good waves! Though it was an exhausting and frustrating surf session, I remember exiting the Atlantic Ocean feeling exhilarated. I knew that it had been worth my time. The fact that I had simply paddled out resulted in stoke.

Experiencing success in sharing our faith is similar to this story of my recent surf session. If we simply try to point others to Jesus and initiate with them, then we have had a successful witnessing experience. I remember coming home from campus one day at UC Santa Barbara and being frustrated with a conversation I had with a student. All the student wanted to do was argue with me. I simply wanted him to understand how he could make a decision to follow Jesus, if he ever wanted to. As I shared this with my roommate at the time and how I felt as if I had failed, he looked at me and said, "Shane, successful witnessing is simply taking the initiative in the power of God's spirit and leaving the results to God. You don't change anyone's mind; you simply have a conversation."

Think about that for a minute. Being successful as a witness and ambassador simply means initiating with people in the power of the Holy Spirit, pointing them to Jesus, and leaving whatever comes next to God. This definition definitely takes the pressure off, doesn't it?

After all, we are not responsible for how people respond to us or to Jesus. We are not called to argue anyone into a relationship with God, to change anyone's mind, or to convince them of anything. Remember what a witness does? We simply share what we have seen, what we have heard, and what we have experienced. "We initiate in a respectful way and leave the results to God." That is successful witnessing!

Questions for
Personal or Group Reflection

1. What does sharing our faith mean?

2. What is your motivator?

3. What is the key to sharing your faith? And who will you share with?

4. What makes a successful witnessing experience?

chapter
eight
Surfers are Servants

"Anyone can make a splash. Jesus makes waves. Don't make a splash with Jesus. Make waves."

Leonard Sweet

At seventeen years of age, in 1978, a cocky and tremendously talented young Californian made the finals of the most popular surf contest in the world - the Pipeline Masters. Taking place on Oahu's famous North Shore, this contest was typically dominated by surfers from Hawaii. The surfing world stood up and took notice of this rising star as he placed behind winner Larry Blair and local star Gerry Lopez.

Joey Buran, known as the "California Kid," was just a teenager when the world took notice of his dominating run through the Pipeline Masters. Buran went on to have a successful career as a professional surfer, placing in the world Top 16 several times. He won the prestigious Katin Pro, the Waimea Pro in Brazil, and placed high in various contests around the world. I remember following the blonde surfer in surfing magazines throughout my youth.

In 1984, Buran once again traveled to Hawaii for the Pipeline Masters. Buran was edging toward the twilight of his career. No Californian had ever won this particular contest and he was hardly a favorite to win the crown of Pipeline Master. No one believed he could win the contest.

No one except for Buran himself. He didn't think he could win. He knew he could win.

The morning of the contest opened with solid fifteen foot surf. Buran tore through the early heats and then the final, beating the world's best surfers. Australians Mark Occhilupo, Tom Carroll and Wayne Bartholomew, and Hawaiian legend and favorite Derek Ho fell to the fiery California Kid.

As he collected his trophy and winner's check on the podium of the biggest contest in the surfing world, Buran proclaimed that "dreams come true." However, several minutes later, a local storm suddenly blew through the event area, people scattered, and Buran was left alone on the sand. Feeling depressed and aimless, Buran flew home and wondered if his life pursuit, what he had been chasing for years, was worthy of his life. According to Buran, it meant nothing. To make a long and exciting story short, he met Jesus Christ and his life was radically changed (for more on his story see resources in the Index).

Since becoming a Christian, Buran has pastored several churches on both the East and West Coasts of the United States, helped countless people in his ministry, and is actively involved in surf coaching. He is the head coach of the US Olympic Surf Team for the 2020 Olympic Games in Tokyo, Japan.

I've always admired Buran as a leader - he is an influencer of people who has impacted many lives around the world. As I've followed his career and ministry throughout the years, there is one defining quality that marks his life: he is a servant. Joey Buran is a good leader because he serves people so well. That's what leadership is: servanthood. Surfers are servants, they help people and Buran models this as well as anyone.

Fish Tacos and Following Jesus

"Shane, let's go, just you and me, bro'," my friend Tim, an older college student during my freshman year, said. He had asked me if I wanted to go for a quick "session" south of the border to Northern Baja, Mexico. As I grew up in Southern California, running to Mexico for a day trip of surfing–and eating a ridiculous amount of locally caught fish tacos–had become a norm.

Gosh, I miss those fish tacos.

As I think back to all of my experiences and relationships I had in college, I think of the tremendous impact Tim had on me. Why? Simply put, Tim was a fantastic leader. Tim had some solid skills. He was a pretty dynamic guy. He had good grades, a great personality, and was quite the "people person." Tim was also a very good surfer.

Over twenty-five years later, when I think of Tim, I don't remember a whole lot about his skills (though I do remember his good surfing!). However, there is one thing I do remember very, very clearly. Tim loved and followed Jesus Christ.

I have recently been reminded of what is so important, so vital, in leading/serving others. Is it a good "up-front" presence? Knowledge? Speaking or debating skills? Education? Charisma?

These are nice, but not what make a good leader.

The Key to Leadership: Think of Leading as Following

Really, being a leader can be quite plain and simple, as my friend Tim modeled to me. Being a good leader is all about being a good follower and a good servant.

My friend wrote a book a few years ago about this concept of leadership that we all can apply. In *I Am a Follower*, Dr. Leonard Sweet simplifies leadership for me: "We have been told our entire lives that we should be leaders, leaders, leaders. But the truth is that the greatest way to create a movement is

Being a good leader is all about being a good follower and a good servant.

to be a follower and to show others how to follow. Following is the most underrated form of leadership in existence" (page 24).

Think about it. This takes the pressure off, doesn't it? If I am going to be fruitful in leading people in any capacity, then I must focus on following. If I'm a good follower and pursue Jesus, then I can be a good leader.

As a parent, coach, Bible study leader, student, spouse, employer, or employee, you are leading and serving in all kinds of ways. Whatever position or "title" you have, God can use you to impact people for Jesus Christ.

The north shore of Oahu is known to have the best waves in the world. Known as the "Seven Mile Miracle," this stretch of beach is the global proving ground of surfing and full of incredible waves when the swell is right. When I was asked to teach at a student conference for the University of Hawaii that was to be held on the "North Shore" (I know, what a tough job), I jumped at the opportunity.

When I landed, our local team leader, a good friend Kent Matsui picked me up at the airport and drove me straight to the first wave on the North Shore: Laniakea. "Lanis" is the first break you come to when driving from the busy city of Honolulu. It is typically a crowded spot to surf. As we came over the hill and I saw Laniakea for the first time, my jaw dropped. The waves were a solid but playful three to five feet, the wind was light providing glassy conditions, and we had three hours until the conference started.

Waves are Toys from God

Clay Marzo is a talented professional surfer from the island of Maui. I once heard Marzo say that "waves are toys from God." This particular day at Laniakea, we had many toys to play with; it felt like we were on a liquid playground with a three-hour recess. As Kent and I shared toys that weekend, I mean waves, I was struck with the kindness, charm, and hospitality of the Hawaiian culture. Kent and his family are great examples of this and I was the fortunate recipient.

I have admired these team leaders for years as they have given their time and vocation to reaching young people there in Hawaii and Asia. What makes my friends such good leaders? They love and follow Jesus.

The Matsuis, who now live and serve on the big island of Hawaii, have relational abilities and skills. But it's not these things they necessarily focus on to help them be fruitful servant-leaders. So, what is it? I've finally figured it out. It's

Focus on walking with God, focus on following him, and you will be a good leader.

their desire to walk humbly with and follow Jesus. Focus on walking with God, focus on following him, and you will be a good leader.

Often times, I complicate leadership. Yes, it's important to think about how I can best steward what God has given me and how to best develop my passions and gifts. I believe God wants me to develop professionally, to attend conferences and workshops, and to be a better communicator. However, these should not be a substitute for growing in my relationship with God and following him.

I think of how surfers all over the world are leading and influencing people. If you look deeper at how these people are impacting others, it's through their servanthood. Some organizations and ministries who are making a difference are Walking on Water, Surfers Healing, Christian Surfers Association, the Mauli Ola Foundation, Waves for Water, and Surfers for Autism. More information on these life-changing ministries, and how you can be involved in serving with them, is found in the index.

I like to think about how I can lead and serve others toward knowing God. It's a relief to know that it's not all about what I do, what my position or title is, or any skills I may possess. Sure, God can and will hopefully use those. But I've learned that it really comes down to following Jesus.

Myths of Leadership

Having served as a minister for over twenty-five years, I've seen my fair share of leadership failures. As I reflect back on where I have fallen short as a leader, as a servant, I find that I, at times, operate from several myths of leadership. I like to call these myths: "What not to do to influence those around you."

What Not to Do In Leading Others

One day, after surfing a beach-break near UC Santa Barbara, I came home to some disturbing news about a friend of mine. As I washed out my wetsuit and hung it in the shower (my wife never liked my wetsuit in the shower), I became more and more angry. I would like to say I sat down and prayed about the situation, how to best handle it, and seek counsel as I considered my next steps. Well, I did not handle it well. My friend came over and it went something like this:

"Are you serious?" I shouted. "Did you really do that and then lie to me?" My friend looked at me with hurt and confused eyes, slammed the door, and walked away. He walked out of my apartment and out of my life. I was numb. Did that really happen? A student and close friend I had mentored for several years had made some poor decisions and I had just confronted him. My confronting him on his actions was hardly done well. I was only making things worse by the way I was handling it (or mishandling it). If I could go back to that situation, I would do it very, very differently. Have you ever said that?

Fast forward almost ten years. I had just surfed a fun beachbreak in Oceanside and was driving south to meet with my friend. I was nervous as I walked into Pizza Port in Carlsbad. We locked eyes immediately. As I walked closer, both of us had tears welling in our eyes. After an awkward handshake, I told him I was very sorry for how poorly I had handled the situation as a friend and as a leader so many years before. I shared how I realized that I had created some of the mess by the way I mishandled the situation we struggled through almost a decade earlier.

He forgave me and we are friends today. I would like to say our friendship is the same as it was before, but it is not. Some of the differences in our relationship stem simply from life changing over the years, but some likely from how I mishandled our conflict. I wish I would have done things differently, but I have learned from it.

When life gets messy around those we serve and lead, and it always does, why do we make it worse by the way we handle it? Has this happened to you? I have been a servant-leader in full-time Christian work for over twenty-five years and I realize that though I am supposed to help people with their problems, I can sometimes make them even worse by mishandling them. How can we serve and lead those around us, especially when mistakes are made, in a healthy manner?

I believe the answer lies in how we view leadership. I have been able to identify several myths, and I have even more than I write below, that I buy into as a leader. As I speak to and mentor other leaders, I realize I am not alone. Below are my myths of leadership.

Myth # 1 Leaders Have It Together

It was past midnight and I was up again. My heart rate was alarmingly high, I was sweating, and I knew sleep would not happen again this night. What was wrong with me? I made several trips to my physician over the previous month and a ridiculous amount of tests and I was finally told that my constant fatigue, rapid heart rate, and sleeplessness were due to depression and an anxiety disorder. As my doctor shared this with me, I literally began to argue with him, "What? No, Doc, you've got it wrong. I've got my stuff together." I couldn't accept what my doctor, a medical professional, was saying about the state of my emotional well-being. I thought that I could not be anxious or depressed because I'm a leader. I help others with their problems. I can handle my own problems. I cast my anxieties on the Lord (1 Peter 5:6-7), I can just pray for peace (Philippians 4:8) and God will work it out. Isn't that how it is supposed to work?

Despite these constant prayers, for the first time in my life, I felt on an emotional and physical level, completely broken. I had not gone surfing for months, which was a testament to how bad I was feeling.

I struggled during that time because I've always bought into the myth that leaders should always look good. They appear put together because they are put together well. Leaders feel good and they help others feel good. They don't have problems. And, when they do, they solve them quickly and easily.

Right?

Wrong.

Here is a challenge for you: Show me a leader in the Bible that is put together well—a leader that is not broken. Keep thinking. David? No, King David slayed his giants, but he was also a murderer and adulterer. Jesus' disciple Peter, whom Jesus built the church upon? No again. Peter denied Christ three times, cut off a servant's ear, and was an emotional roller-coaster throughout his time with Jesus. How about the great Apostle Paul? The same guy who wrote more than half of the New Testament. Surely, he had has life put together well, right? No. Paul hunted down and persecuted followers of Jesus before he became a Christian. In his own words, as he wrote to his friend Timothy, Paul said, *"Here is a trustworthy saying that deserves full acceptance: Christ Jesus came into the world to save sinners—of whom I am the worst"* (I Timothy 1:15).

When I finally began to grasp the fact that I was, indeed, a very broken leader, I was even more aware of God's grace and healing power. As I opened up to God, friends, and family I realized that God uses broken people. God used broken people throughout the Bible, and he uses broken people today.

Myth # 2 If I Could Just Lead Like Him or Her

Have you ever thought, "Wow, if I could speak up front like that person?" Or, "What if I could just have their confidence in sharing God?" I say it all the time. Over the last few years though, I realize that God has made me to serve, to lead and influence in a unique way. When I try to be someone I am not, I only short-circuit how God can use me to minister to and impact others. Comparison never ends well for anyone. Take it from me, one who has been comparing for years.

I am reminded of a great leader in the Old Testament. Jeremiah was called by God to lead in a nation (Judah) that was very wicked. God actually calls Jeremiah to be his servant to not just Judah, but to the surrounding nations.

Below is the conversation between God and Jeremiah:

> *The word of the Lord came to me, saying, "Before I*
> *formed you in the womb I knew you, before you were*

born I set you apart; I appointed you as a prophet to the nations." "Alas, Sovereign Lord," I said, "I do not know how to speak; I am too young." But the Lord said to me, "Do not say, 'I am too young.' You must go to everyone I send you to and say whatever I command you. Do not be afraid of them, for I am with you and will rescue you," declares the Lord. Then the Lord reached out his hand and touched my mouth and said to me, "I have put my words in your mouth. See, today I appoint you over nations and kingdoms to uproot and tear down, to destroy and overthrow, to build and to plant (Jeremiah 1:4-10).

As I read this interaction between God and a leader, I was impressed with Jeremiah's heart toward God. Yes, he was afraid of what God was asking him to do. He didn't have a proven track record of great skills. In fact, Jeremiah actually complains to God, *"Behold I cannot speak"*(1:6). God was calling Jeremiah to a public ministry, to speak, to be in front of people. Jeremiah responds with an excuse. God responds to Jeremiah with wods of power and encouragement: *"Behold I have put my words in your mouth"* (1:9).

Myth # 3 A Leader Always Has a Fresh Walk with God

Recently, I had breakfast with a friend of mine. Steve has been in a neighborhood Bible study that I lead with my wife. We have been in this group and doing life together for over 5 years. I was hesitant to share with Steve some things I was struggling with. Finally, I told Steve that I was not "feeling it" in my relationship with God. I was not talking so much about emotions, but simply that I had not been connecting with God very much recently.

Steve's response was eye-opening, "Shane, I've known you for five years and honestly, this is the first time I have even been able to relate to you." As I said, I have led Steve for quite a while and I thought we knew each other very well. Boy, was I wrong!

Steve shared that he always thought my relationship with God was fresh and exciting. It made sense he would believe this as I never shared otherwise.

I have looked far and wide for people in God's word who are perfect and always had a fresh relationship with Jesus. Keep looking—you won't find one.

God Can Use Anyone

Jonah is a story most of us know. Jonah is called by God to go to Nineveh and warn the nation, to tell them to turn from their wicked ways. Instead of obeying God, Jonah jumps in a boat and literally sails in the opposite direction. We hear it from parents and Sunday School teachers. We hear how this guy Jonah gets eaten by a fish (my kids correct me that a whale is not a fish, thank you very much) and thrown up three days later. End of story?

Not at all. Take a moment and read Jonah. For now, I'll summarize what you will later read:

Jonah 1: *Arise, go to Nineveh, that great city, and cry out against it, for their wickedness has come up before Me. But Jonah arose to flee to Tarshish from the presence of the Lord* (Jonah 1:2-3, NASB). God commands Jonah to go and warn the people of Nineveh to turn from their wickedness. Jonah immediately jumps on a boat that is going in the opposite direction.

Jonah 2: Jonah can't run from God, though he does a good job of trying. Jonah is thrown over the ship by the sailors who know he has done something to displease God. After Jonah is tossed into the sea, a great fish swallows him. Inside the belly of the fish, Jonah comes to terms with his own sin. *Then the Lord had prepared a great fish to swallow Jonah....Then Jonah prayed to the Lord his God from the fish's belly, And he said, "I cried out to the Lord because of my affliction, and He answered me"* (Jonah 1:17, 2:1, NKJV).

Jonah 3: This chapter is an example of God using a flawed leader. God calls Jonah again to go to Nineveh and this time, Jonah obeys. *So Jonah arose and went to Nineveh, according to the word of the Lord....So the people of Nineveh believed God* (Jonah 3:1,5 ESV).

Jonah 4: The final chapter of this brief book does not end with a bow on it. We see Jonah revert back to a state of self-centeredness after God saves the city. *Then God saw their works, that they turned from their evil way; and God relented from the disaster that He had said He would bring upon them, and He did not do it. But it displeased Jonah exceedingly, and he became angry* (Jonah 3:10, 4:1, NKJV).

Here are just a few observations of this leader God used:

• Jonah runs: Does Jonah respond with a great leader attitude when God calls? Does he go after God's calling with undaunted courage? Hardly. He actually flees in the other direction. That's like saying if God called you to serve him in Uruguay and you ran off to Iceland.

- The only character in this story that does not obey God is Jonah: The fish, the sailors, the vine, the wind and waves, and even the worm all obey God. Jonah, this leader God has called, does not.
- God uses this flawed leader to save others: *Then the people in Nineveh believed in God* (Jonah 3:5, ESV).

I like Jonah because he is a model of someone God uses who is hardly perfect. I think Jonah is the perfect portrait of a leader—not a perfect leader—as he is someone not too high of a hero for us to identify with. As Eugene Peterson says, "He is a companion to our ineptness."

The Bible is full of leaders like Jonah: insecure, unfit, some are quite young, and all are broken. God uses all of this to glorify himself and spread his name. Jonah didn't always do things right, but God used him in great ways. God wants to use you for great things, too.

Questions for
Personal or Group Reflection

1. Do you have your own myths of leadership?

2. How have you defined "leader" in the past? How does the Bible define a leader?

3. How can you serve those around you? How can you lead as a servant?

4. As you serve others, what myth of leadership are you buying into that may be short-circuiting how God can use you?

chapter
nine

Keep Paddling

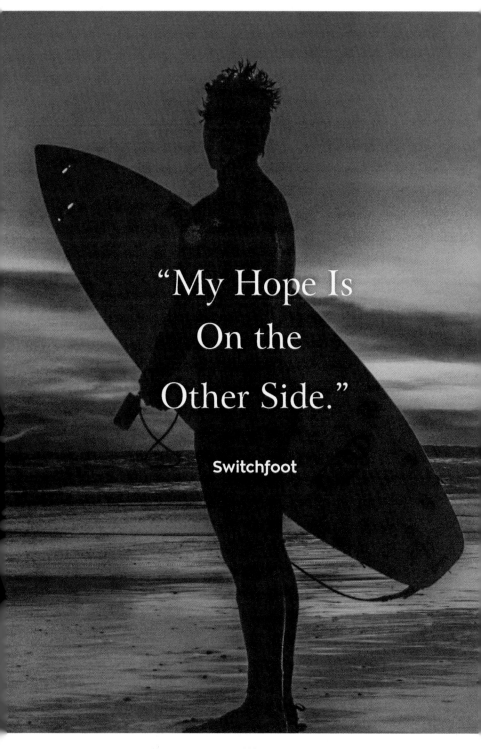

"My Hope Is On the Other Side."

Switchfoot

It was the second day of a much anticipated and long prepared for trip to El Salvador. One of my best friends and I had been saving and planning for this surfing trip for well over a year. For months, I had been training for the long paddles and extra-long surf sessions. I was stoked to be surfing perfect waves with a good friend.

After two hours of overhead waves, I paddled far outside to wait for a bigger set. After a few minutes, a solid five footer approached. I turned my board to shore, dropped in and sped down the line. After a few carves, I raced to the inside. At the end of the wave, my front foot slipped and I wiped out, face-planted, and tumbled down with the lip of the wave.

With all of my speed as I wiped out, I didn't actually penetrate the water. Instead, I sort of skipped down the wave. As soon as I hit the water, I felt a numbing, tingling, and sharp pain in my right shoulder. I remember thinking, "Uh oh, this can't be good." As I poked my head up for air, the wave picked me up again and threw me "over the falls." Think of being in a washing machine with little breath—this best describes going over the falls.

The wave finally let me go and I surfaced with my right shoulder dislocated. I was a good quarter-mile from the boat (there are no roads to this break so we hired a boat to drive us), waves were approaching, and my arm and shoulder felt as if they were on fire. After a minute or so, I was able to pop my shoulder back into place, limp back to the boat, and was taken back to the camp. After several hours at the hospital, I caught a taxi-cab back to the hotel. As we bounced, quite literally, on the bumpy roads, I thought of my dream trip now becoming a big disappointment. All the time, money, and effort spent was now crashing down on just the second day of the trip. I immediately called the airlines and was on a flight bound for home, bound for many doctor's appointments, physical therapy, and who knows how much time out of the water.

I was discouraged, defeated, and disappointed. This was hardly what I signed up for when I planned the trip.

Life throws discouragement, defeat, and disappointment all too often. In fact, life is often more about living in challenging circumstances and hard times than in the good times. *Dropping In* has hopefully been a source of encouragement to you as you seek to grow in a relationship with God and others. As we wrap up our time together, I want to encourage you to keep

---

Keep paddling even when times are difficult.

---

paddling even when times are difficult. When things become "dislocated," how do we continue to paddle toward God and others?

The answer lies in our perspective. A perspective is a point of view, a particular way of thinking. Having the right perspective, having an eternal perspective, means that we evaluate our values, events, beliefs, actions and decisions from God's point of view. Living with an eternal perspective means we use God's values as we evaluate our own lives. Having an eternal perspective means that we recognize that everything we do now, in the present, has an eternal consequence and should be evaluated within that perspective. We view the world through "spiritual eyes," with God's perspective. Or, we can simply view the world through my "physical eyes" and fail to view the eternal. Our view of life will significantly impact our actions and decisions.

Apple Computers started in the 1970s by two young men in their garage – Steve Wozniak and Steve Jobs. Wozniak was a technical genius; Jobs was all about the big picture and vision. Jobs had a grand vision of literally changing the world with what he considered "insanely great" computers. He had a passion for Macintosh.

There's a story I often tell about how Steve Jobs coaxed the president of the Pepsi Corporation to leave his very secure and very well-paying job to come work for this upstart company, to come to work for Macintosh. Jobs asked John Sculley of Pepsi to meet with him, gave him a recruiting talk, and told him of the great need to create and sell computers. However, the Pepsi executive wasn't willing to leave behind his future of power and wealth. Not willing to accept a "no," Jobs looked at Sculley and said these famous lines, "Do you want to spend the rest of your life selling sugar water, or do you want a chance to change the world?" With that question ringing in his ears, Sculley left Pepsi and came to work for Apple Computers.

I think we all have a desire to make a difference with our life and to invest in something that really matters. We don't want to spend our lives only selling "sugar water." We want to invest in things that matter and will impact the world. God encourages us to think about our life from the standpoint of eternity, to ponder and invest in the things that are eternal.

In fact, it's when we lose sight of the eternal things that we often lose our way in life, becoming only focused on the present. Time passes and before long, we realize – like John Sculley of Pepsi – that we are only making "sugar water."

Having the right perspective will help as we go through the

challenges of life and ultimately grow us more toward God. These verses in the Bible help me think and live with an eternal perspective:

> *If then you have been raised with Christ, seek the things that are above, where Christ is, seated at the right hand of God. Set your minds on things that are above, not on things that are on earth. For you have died, and your life is hidden with Christ in God. When Christ who is your life appears, then you also will appear with him in glory* (Colossians 3:1-4, ESV).

Focus on the Eternal

When I lived on the central coast of California, I was asked to perform a funeral for a student who had tragically been killed. As I prepared to speak at the service celebrating the life of this young man, I couldn't help but think of my own mortality. I asked myself, "What was I living for? What would I want to be placed on my tombstone?" And, "Are my time and talents being invested in things that will outlive me?"

As I prayed for this person's family and evaluated my own life, I was reminded that there are only three things in life that are eternal: the Bible, God and our relationship with Him, and the souls of men and women. Living with this truth in mind is living with an eternal perspective.

What are some of those "things above" that we can live for? What are the things the Bible says are eternal and worthy of our investment? Here are a few:

1. God's word is eternal (Matthew 5:17-18). The writings of every other teacher or great philosopher will fade, but the wisdom of God in Scripture will always remain.

2. God is eternal and our relationship with Him is the only relationship that is eternal (John 10:27-31).

3. Souls of men and women are eternal – all people will spend eternity in either Heaven or Hell (John 3:16-18, 36; Luke 16:19-31; 2 Thess. 1:5-12).

The Bible is clear on what to focus on that is eternal: living for Him and others. In college, one of my favorite bands was Nirvana. Nirvana has the best song in the history of songs, *Smells Like Teen Spirit*. I remember, before and after class, after work, especially before going surfing, even on my way home from Bible study, and pretty much everywhere else, I listened to that song.

I also remember having no idea what Nirvana was singing about–the more I listened, the murkier the song seemed. Nirvana was loud, but they were hardly clear in their message.

Fortunately, God is much clearer about the message–the story–of the Bible. From the very beginning of Genesis all the way through the book of Revelation, we see the obvious theme of the Bible: God's love for all people (including you!), and his desire to bless all people.

Another word for bless is the word heal. One of my professors in seminary, David McDonald, says that God desires to use us to heal others. He once said to me that we, as God's followers, are all about healing. "The church is an agency of healing. We continue the mission of Jesus, picking up where he left off. We are the body of Christ and each one of us has a role to play in cultivating God's kingdom on earth." I like the idea of helping heal people. Helping people is living with an eternal perspective.

Be Careful of the Temporal

One of my favorite Australian surfers is Joel Parkinson. "Parko" is a world champion and known the world over for his smooth style and years of surfing in the World Surf League. I once heard Parko speak of figuring out what really matters after surfing his whole life, "It's funny because you think surfing is your whole life, but then when you make a family, it seems like it's not at all." Parkinson understands that as fun and enjoyable as surfing can be and as special as it is to so many of us, it's not what is most important. The Bible has this to say about the temporal:

> *Do not store up for yourselves treasures on earth, where moth and rust destroy, and where thieves break in and steal. But store up for yourselves treasures in heaven* (Matthew 6:19-20a, NASB).

> *The world is passing away, and also its lusts; but the one who does the will of God lives forever* (I John 2:15-18, NASB).

> *Our life is like a vapor; it appears for a little while and then vanishes away* (James 4:13-14, NASB).

We all make New Year's resolutions. One of the most common is, "I'm finally going to begin a savings account next year. I'll start after January 1st." Here is what we imply when we make that statement: I value preparing for the future, but I'm too concerned with today's problems to really do anything about it.

If we don't live intentionally and without an eternal perspective, this can become our life story. Right now (not January 1st) is when we need to save for the future: living for God and his word and investing in those things that are eternal.

Have the Right Anchor

It was barely five o'clock on a mid-winter morning. The air temperature was a chilly 42 degrees, the water temperature no more than 53 degrees. The swell was northwest at a solid four to six feet. This is the day of surfing we dreamed about all year. We stood in waist deep water as we timed the waves, launched the small Zodiac (a small, inflatable, and rigid boat) over the last set, and motored up to paradise.

Paradise in my terms is defined as "The Ranch." Hollister Ranch is an undeveloped stretch of pristine coastline northwest of Santa Barbara, sitting just below Point Conception (Central California). Access to this stretch of amazing surfing is very limited and all but impossible, if you don't own land on the Ranch.

Unless you have a boat. Fortunately, one of my good buddies had a boat.

After cruising at twenty knots for twenty minutes, we pulled up to the first series of right-hand point and reef-breaks. After scrambling to wax our boards, fasten our leashes, and drink the last ounces of precious coffee, we jumped off the side of the Zodiac and paddled to the waves.

Oh, and one more thing before we jumped into the ocean;

we never, ever would forget to drop the anchor. The most important pre-surf ritual was to drop the anchor. Without the anchor, our small boat would drift away, leaving us with no way home. Without the anchor, our food and water, dry clothing, and transportation home would be lost. Without the anchor, the boat would drift aimlessly at the mercy of the wind and waves.

We need an anchor for our lives as desperately as we needed an anchor for our Zodiac. Christ provides that anchor. Christ, as our anchor, protects us from the waves and the winds of life,

---

With Jesus Christ as our anchor, we are able to live with an eternal perspective.

---

whether those are doubts, fears, or outward circumstances. With Jesus Christ as our anchor, we are able to live with an eternal perspective.

One of the more influential and talented bands today is Switchfoot, led by Jon Foreman and his brother Tim. This band has been influencing the world since the late 1990s and have sold millions of albums. Jon and Tim are both good surfers and named themselves after a surfing term. When asked about the name "Switchfoot," Jon Foreman says that, "We all love to surf and have been surfing all our lives. So to us, the name made sense. To switch your feet means to take a new stance facing the opposite direction. It's about change and movement, a different way of approaching life and music."

In one of their more popular songs, Switchfoot writes of where our hope is anchored:

> *I can feel it building up inside*
> *The images that play inside my mind*
> *The dreams that I've been dreaming all my life*
> *The colors that live outside of the lines*
>
> *But dreams aren't all I hide beneath this skin*
> *The cord is cut, the fears and doubts begin*
> *My hope is anchored on the other side*
> *With the colors that live outside of the lines*

Our hope is anchored on the other side. The ultimate reality is not what we see immediately around us—and this shapes our perspective. If we know Christ, we have something we can place our hope and anchor in that is far better than the things around us that don't last.

Having Christ as our anchor helps us realize how short our decades on earth are compared to all of eternity. Our perspective on the things of this world changes; we will have an eternal perspective.

One Final Wave

One of my boys has been working at a surf school in Cocoa Beach, Florida. All day long, David teaches young kids to surf;

he shows them where to walk out to the wet sand. Once in the water, he carefully guides them to the breaking surf, gently pushes them into waves, and over a week's time, helps them grow as young surfers. I remember watching one little girl light up as she jumped to her feet and rode her first wave on her own. Her smile defined her feeling. Over the course of five days, this girl was the definition of the word stoke.

As we started *Dropping In*, I explained that God wants you to experience spiritual stoke. Spiritual stoke means to live as God intended, to live and grow in an abundant and joyful relationship with the creator of the universe. *Dropping In* is meant to help you begin and/or take the next step in spiritual stoke. I am praying this is true for you.

Psalm 93:4 says, *Mightier than the thunders of many waters, mightier than the waves of the sea, the LORD on high is mighty!* (ESV)

As you surf throughout life, may you continue to grow in the understanding that God and his love for you are mightier than any wave, any ocean, any sea.

Now put down the book and I'll see you in the water.

Questions for
Personal or Group Reflection

1. Where are you setting your mind on at this time in your life? Why? Why is it so difficult to keep our minds on things above?

2. Are there any changes you need to make in order to live more for eternity in your everyday life? Changes in what you value? Changes in how you spend your time? Changes in your priorities?

3. When you look back on your life, what things will you want to have accomplished or been true of you?

Additional Resources

Further Your Wave Journey

Shanesebastian.com – Learn more about this book, purchase it for your friends and family, grab a *Dropping In* t-shirt or sticker, read a brief blog post, and get stoked!

Startingwithgod.com – Designed to help a new Christian or a mature Christian grow spiritually.

Cru.org – The purpose of Cru is helping to fulfill the Great Commission in the power of the Holy Spirit by winning people to faith in Jesus Christ. They build them in their faith and sends them to win and build others. They help the body of Christ to do evangelism and discipleship through a variety of creative ways. Go to this website for hundreds of articles, Bible studies, life stories, and other resources to help you wherever you are on your spiritual journey. Also, an excellent tool for topical group or personal Bible studies.

Surfline.com – A great wave forecasting website with plenty of surf intel to grow your passion.

Magicseaweed.com – Similar to the above site.

Walkingonwater.org – Walking On Water is a Christian non-profit organization dedicated to sharing the Gospel of Jesus Christ with this generation's global surfing community since 1995. Go to this site for information on mission opportunities, surf camps, surfing documentaries, and other ways to grow closer to God and others.

Wavesforwater.org – "Get clean water to those who need it." A fantastic and tangible way to serve the practical needs of others while going on a surf trip.

Christiansurfers.com – Christian Surfers wants to help you "Live Life to the Full." The mission of Christian Surfers is to help every surfer and every surf community have the opportunity to experience and follow Jesus Christ.

Surfersforautism.org – The mission for Surfers for Autism is to unlock the potential of people with developmental delays, support advocacy for autism issues and scientific research. Go to this website to learn more of how you can be involved.

Mauliola.org - The Mauli Ola Foundation (MOF) is a nonprofit organization dedicated to providing hope and confidence to individuals living with genetic diseases. Harnessing the healing powers of the ocean, we introduce surfing and ocean-based activities as natural therapies. We are honored to share our knowledge of the ocean, family values and community.

WorshipGeneration.com – this website shares more of the personal journey and ministry of surfer and pastor Joey Buran.

"But mightier than the violent raging of the seas, mightier than the breakers on the shore— the Lord above is mightier than these!"

Psalm 93:4

Surfer pictured: Aaron Gold

photo by Aaron Lynton

"For this is how God loved the world: He gave his one and only Son, so that everyone who believes in him will not perish but have eternal life."

John 3:16

Surfer pictured: Damien Hobgood

photo by Aaron Lynton

167

IF YOU'RE A FAN OF THIS BOOK, WILL YOU HELP ME SPREAD THE WORD?

There are several ways you can help me get the word out about the message of this book...

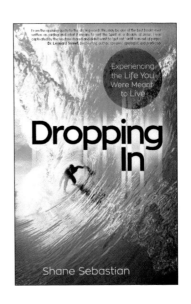

- Post a 5-Star review on Amazon.

- Write about the book on your Facebook, Twitter, Instagram – any social media you regularly use!

- If you blog, consider referencing the book, or publishing an excerpt from the book with a link back to my website. You have my permission to do this as long as you provide proper credit and backlinks.

- Recommend the book to friends – word-of-mouth is still the most effective form of advertising.

- Purchase additional copies to give away as gifts.

- For more information on how to pray and be a part of the Sebastians' ministry, visit give.cru.org/0428848.

The best way to connect with me is by email at: shane.sebastian@cru.org or by Facebook through @droppinginbook.

ENJOY THESE OTHER BOOKS
BY SHANE SEBASTIAN

This Change is Everything
The Hope and Future of
Gospel Mission

In this book, Shane will walk you
through the history of God using
young people to transform individuals,
communities, cultures, and nations.
This book might just change your life.

Packed
Discovering God's Heart for
the Nations

*Through Packed: Discovering God's
Heart for the Nations,* you have the
opportunity to walk through an
exciting 28-day journey that explores
what the Bible says about God's heart
for every people group. This devotional
is the collaboration of fifteen different
men and women who represent various ministry focuses and
different cultural backgrounds.

You can order these books from crupress.com and at
shanesebastian.com or wherever you purchase your favorite
books.